T0203365

Scheduling of Large-scale Virtualized Infrastructures

FOCUS SERIES

Series Editor Narendra Jussien

Scheduling of Large-scale Virtualized Infrastructures

Toward Cooperative Management

Flavien Quesnel

WILEY

First published 2014 in Great Britain and the United States by ISTE Ltd and John Wiley & Sons, Inc.

ISTE Ltd
27-37 St George's Road
London SW19 4EU
UK

www.iste.co.uk

John Wiley & Sons, Inc.
111 River Street
Hoboken, NJ 07030
USA

www.wiley.com

© ISTE Ltd 2014
The rights of Flavien Quesnel to be identified as the author of this work have been asserted by him in accordance with the Copyright, Designs and Patents Act 1988.

Library of Congress Control Number: 2014941926

British Library Cataloguing-in-Publication Data
A CIP record for this book is available from the British Library
ISSN 2051-2481 (Print)
ISSN 2051-249X (Online)
ISBN 978-1-84821-620-4

Printed and bound in Great Britain by CPI Group (UK) Ltd., Croydon, Surrey CR0 4YY

Contents

List of Abbreviations

ACO   Ant Colony Optimization

API   Application Programming Interface

BOINC Berkeley Open Infrastructure for Network Computing

BVT   Borrowed Virtual Time scheduler

CFS   Completely Fair Scheduler

CS   Credit Scheduler

DOS   Distributed Operating System

DVMS   Distributed Virtual Machine Scheduler

EC2   Elastic Compute Cloud

EGEE   Enabling Grids for E-sciencE

EGI   European Grid Infrastructure

I/O   Input/Output

GPOS   General Purpose Operating System

IaaS   Infrastructure as a Service

IP	Internet Protocol
JRE	Java Runtime Environment
JVM	Java Virtual Machine
KSM	Kernel Shared Memory
KVM	Kernel-based Virtual Machine
LHC	Large Hadron Collider
MHz	Megahertz
MPI	Message Passing Interface
NFS	Network File System
NTP	Network Time Protocol
OSG	Open Science Grid
PaaS	Platform as a Service
SaaS	Software as a Service
SCVMM	System Center Virtual Machine Manager
URL	Uniform Resource Locator
VIM	Virtual Infrastructure Manager
VLAN	Virtual Local Area Network
VM	Virtual Machine
WLCG	Worldwide LHC Computing Grid
XSEDE	Extreme Science and Engineering Discovery Environment

Introduction

Context

Nowadays, increasing needs in computing power are satisfied by federating more and more computers (or nodes) to build distributed infrastructures.

Historically, these infrastructures have been managed by means of user-space frameworks [FOS 06, LAU 06] or distributed operating systems [MUL 90, PIK 95, LOT 05, RIL 06, COR 08].

Over the past few years, a new kind of software manager has appeared, managers that rely on system virtualization [NUR 09, SOT 09, VMW 10, VMW 11, APA 12, CIT 12, MIC 12, OPE 12, NIM 13]. System virtualization allows dissociating the software from the underlying node by encapsulating it in a virtual machine [POP 74, SMI 05]. This technology has important advantages for distributed infrastructure providers and users. It has especially favored the emergence of cloud computing, and more specifically of infrastructure as a service. In this model, raw virtual machines are provided to users, who can customize them by installing an operating system and applications.

Problem statement and contributions

These virtual machines are created, deployed on nodes and managed during their entire lifecycle by virtual infrastructure managers (VIMs).

Most of the VIMs are highly centralized, which means that a few dedicated nodes commonly handle the management tasks. Although this approach facilitates some administration tasks and is sometimes required, for example, to have a global view of the utilization of the infrastructure, it can lead to problems. As a matter of fact, centralization limits the scalability of VIMs, in other words their ability to be reactive when they have to manage large-scale virtual infrastructures (tens of thousands of nodes) that are increasingly common nowadays [WHO 13].

In this book, we focus on ways to improve the scalability of VIMs; one of them consists of decentralizing the processing of several management tasks.

Decentralization has already been studied through research on distributed operating systems (DOSs). Therefore, we wondered whether the VIMs could benefit from the results of this research. To answer this question, we compared the management features proposed by VIMs and DOSes at the node level and at the whole infrastructure level [QUE 11]. We first developed the reflections initiated a few years ago [HAN 05, HEI 06, ROS 07], to show that virtualization technologies have benefited from the research on operating systems, and vice versa. We then extended our study to a distributed context.

Comparing VIMs and DOSes enabled us to identify some possible contributions, especially to decentralize the dynamic scheduling of virtual machines. Dynamic scheduling of virtual machines aims to move virtual machines from one node to another when it is necessary, for example (1) to enable a system administrator to perform a maintenance operation or (2) to optimize the utilization of the infrastructure by taking into account the evolution of virtual machines' resource needs. Dynamic scheduling is still uncommonly used by VIMs deployed in production, even though several approaches have been proposed in the scientific literature. However, given the fact that they rely on a centralized model, these approaches face scalability issues and are not able to react quickly when some nodes are overloaded. This can lead to the violation of service level agreements proposed to users, since virtual machines' resource needs are not satisfied for some time.

To mitigate this problem, several proposals have been made to decentralize the dynamic scheduling of virtual machines [BAR 10, YAZ 10, MAR 11, MAS 11, ROU 11, FEL 12b, FEL 12c]. Yet, almost all of the implemented prototypes use some partially centralized mechanisms, and satisfy the needs of reactivity and scalability only to a limited extent.

The contribution of this book lies precisely in this area of research; more specifically, we propose distributed virtual machine scheduler (DVMS), a more decentralized application to dynamically schedule virtual machines hosted on a distributed infrastructure. DVMS is deployed as a network of agents organized following a ring topology, and that also cooperate with one another to process the events (linked to overloaded/underloaded node problems) that occur on the infrastructure as quickly as possible; DVMS can process several events simultaneously and independently by dynamically partitioning the infrastructure, each partition having a size that is appropriate to the complexity of the event to be processed. We optimized the traversal of the ring by defining shortcuts, to enable a message to leave a partition as quickly as possible, instead of crossing each node of this partition. Moreover, we guaranteed that an event would be solved if a solution existed. For this purpose, we let pairs of partitions merge when there is no free node left to be absorbed by a partition that needs to grow to solve its event; it is necessary to make partitions reach a consensus before merging, to avoid deadlocks.

We implemented these concepts through a prototype, which we validated (1) by means of simulations (first with a test framework specifically designed to meet our needs, second with the SimGrid toolkit [CAS 08]) and (2) with the help of real world experiments on the Grid'5000 test bed [GRI 13] (using Flauncher [BAL 12] to configure the nodes and the virtual machines). We observed that

DVMS was particularly reactive to manage virtual infrastructures involving several tens of thousands of virtual machines distributed across thousands of nodes; as a matter of fact, DVMS needed approximately 1 s to find a solution to the problem linked with an overloaded node, where other prototypes could require several minutes.

Once the prototype had been validated [QUE 12, QUE 13], we focused on the future work on DVMS, and especially on:

– Defining new events corresponding to virtual machine submissions or maintenance operations on a node;

– Adding fault-tolerance mechanisms, so that scheduling can go on even if a node crashes;

– Taking account of the network topology to build partitions, to let nodes communicate efficiently even if they are linked with one another by a wide area network. The final goal will be to implement a full decentralized VIM. This goal should be reached by the discovery [LEB 12] initiative, which will leverage this work.

Structure of this book

The remainder of this book is structured as follows.

Part 1: management of distributed infrastructures

The first part deals with distributed infrastructures.

In Chapter 1, we present the main types of distributed infrastructures that exist nowadays, and the software frameworks that are traditionally used to manage them.

In Chapter 2, we introduce virtualization and explain its advantages to manage and use distributed infrastructures.

In Chapter 3, we focus on the features and limitations of the main virtual infrastructure managers.

Part 2: toward a cooperative and decentralized framework to manage virtual infrastructures

The second part is a study of the components that are necessary to build a cooperative and decentralized framework to manage virtual infrastructures.

In Chapter 4, we investigate the similarities between virtual infrastructure managers and the frameworks that are traditionally used to manage distributed infrastructures; moreover, we identify some possible contributions, mainly on virtual machine scheduling.

In Chapter 5, we focus on the latest contributions on decentralized dynamic scheduling of virtual machines.

Part 3: DVMS, a cooperative and decentralized framework to dynamically schedule virtual machines

The third part deals with DVMS, a cooperative and decentralized framework to dynamically schedule virtual machines.

In Chapter 6, we present the theory behind DVMS and the implementation of the prototype.

In Chapter 7, we detail the experimental protocol and the tools used to evaluate and validate DVMS.

In Chapter 8, we analyze the experimental results.

In Chapter 9, we describe future work.

PART 1

Management of Distributed Infrastructures

Distributed Infrastructures Before the Rise of Virtualization

Organizations having huge needs in computing power can use either powerful mainframes or federations of less powerful computers (called nodes), which are part of distributed infrastructures. The latter solution has become increasingly popular over the past few years; this can be explained by the fact that: (1) a federation of nodes is cheaper than a mainframe for the same computing power and (2) a federation involving a huge number of nodes is more powerful than a mainframe.

In this chapter, we present the main kinds of distributed infrastructures and we focus on their management from the software point of view. In particular, we give an overview of the frameworks that were designed to manage these infrastructures before virtualization became popular.

1.1. Overview of distributed infrastructures

The first distributed infrastructures to appear were clusters; data centers, grids and volunteer computing platforms then followed (see Figure 1.1).

1.1.1. *Cluster*

The unit generally used in distributed infrastructures is the cluster.

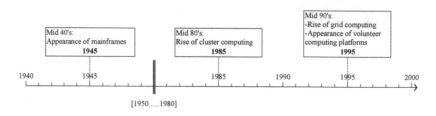

Figure 1.1. *Order of appearance of the main categories of distributed infrastructures*

DEFINITION 1.1.– Cluster – *A cluster is a federation of homogeneous nodes, that is to say all nodes are identical, to facilitate their maintenance as well as their utilization. These nodes are close to one another (typically the same room) and are linked by means of a high-performance local area network.*

1.1.2. *Data center*

Clusters can be grouped inside a federation, for example a data center.

DEFINITION 1.2.– Data Center – *A data center is a kind of federation of clusters, where these clusters are close to one another (typically the same building or group of buildings) and communicate through a local area network.*

The characteristics of the nodes can vary from one cluster to another, especially if these clusters were not built at the same date. Each cluster has its own network; network performance can differ from one network to another.

1.1.3. *Grid*

Clusters and data centers belonging to several organizations sharing a common goal can be pooled to build a more powerful infrastructure, called grid.

DEFINITION 1.3.– Grid – *A grid is a distributed infrastructure that "enable(s) resource sharing and coordinated problem solving in dynamic, multi-institutional virtual organizations" [FOS 08].*

A grid is generally made of heterogeneous nodes.

Moreover, the components of a grid communicate by means of a wide area network, whose performance is worse than a local area network; this is especially true for the latency (that is to say the time required to transmit a message between two distant nodes), and sometimes also for the bandwidth (in other words, the maximum amount of data that can be transferred between two distant nodes per unit of time).

There are many grids. Some of them are nationwide, like Grid'5000 [GRI 13] and the infrastructure managed by France Grilles [FRA 13] in France, or FutureGrid [FUT 13], Open Science Grid (OSG) [OSG 13] and Extreme Science and Engineering Discovery Environment (XSEDE, previously TeraGrid) [XSE 13] in the USA. Others were implemented on a whole continent, by leveraging nationwide grids, like the European Grid Infrastructure (EGI, formerly – Enabling Grids for E-sciencE (EGEE)) [EGI 13] in Europe. Finally, other grids are worldwide, like the Worldwide LHC Computing Grid (WLCG) [WIC 13] that relies especially on OSG and EGI to analyze data from the Large Hadron Collider (LHC) of the European Center for Nuclear Research (CERN).

1.1.4. *Volunteer computing platforms*

Pooled resources belonging to individuals rather than organization are the building blocks for volunteer computing platforms.

DEFINITION 1.4.– Volunteer Computing Platform – *A volunteer computing platform is similar to a grid, except that it is composed of heterogeneous nodes made available by volunteers (not necessarily organizations) that are typically linked through the Internet.*

Berkeley Open Infrastructure for Network Computing (BOINC) [AND 04] is an example of such a platform. It aims to federate Internet users around different research projects, like

SETI@home [SET 13]. The goal of SETI@home is to analyze radio communications from space, searching for extra-terrestrial intelligence. Internet users simply need to download the BOINC application and join the project they want to take part in; when they do not use their computer, the application automatically fetches some tasks (for example, computations to perform or data to analyze) from the aforementioned project, processes them and then submits the results to the project.

XtremWeb [FED 01] is an application that allows building a platform that is similar to BOINC. However, contrary to BOINC, it allows the tasks that are distributed across the computers of several users to communicate directly with one another.

1.2. Distributed infrastructure management from the software point of view

The management of the aforementioned distributed infrastructures requires taking account of several concerns, especially the connection of users to the system and their identification, submission of tasks, scheduling, deployment, monitoring and termination. These concerns may involve several kinds of resources (see Figure 1.2):

- access nodes, for user's connections;
- one or several node(s) dedicated to infrastructure management;
- storage nodes, for user's data;
- worker nodes, to process the tasks submitted by users.

1.2.1. Secured connection to the infrastructure and identification of users

In order to use the infrastructure, users first need to connect to it [LAU 06, COR 08, GRI 13].

This connection can be made in several ways. From the hardware point of view, users may use a private network or the Internet; moreover, they may be authorized to connect to every node of the infrastructure, or only to dedicated nodes (the access nodes). From the software point of view, it is mandatory to decide which application and which protocol to use; this choice is critical to the security of the infrastructure, to identify users, to determine which resources they can have access to and for how much time, to take account of the resources they have used so far and to prevent a malicious user to steal resources or data from another user.

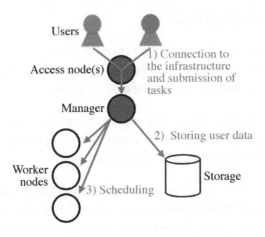

Figure 1.2. *Organization of a distributed infrastructure*

1.2.2. *Submission of tasks*

Once connected to the infrastructure, users should be able to submit tasks [LAU 06, COR 08, GRI 13].

For this purpose, they have to specify the characteristics of tasks, depending on the functionalities provided by the infrastructure:

– programs and/or data required to process the tasks; if necessary, users should be able to upload them to the infrastructure;

– required resources, from a qualitative and quantitative point of view, and the duration of use; users may also mention whether their tasks can be processed in a degraded mode, that is to say with less resources than what they asked for;

– the date/time processing must start and end;

– links between tasks (if applicable), and possible precedence constraints, that specify that some tasks have be processed before others; when tasks are linked with one another, the infrastructure manager has to execute coherent actions on these tasks; this is done during scheduling.

1.2.3. *Scheduling of tasks*

DEFINITION 1.5.– Scheduling – *Scheduling is the process of assigning resources to tasks, in order to process them [ROT 94, TAN 01, LEU 04, STA 08]. Scheduling is performed by a scheduler.*

Scheduling has to take account of the aforementioned characteristics of tasks: required resources, start/end date/time, priority, links between tasks, etc. Scheduling may be static or dynamic.

DEFINITION 1.6.– Static Scheduling – *Scheduling is said to be static when each task remains on the same worker node when it is processed. The initial placement of tasks takes account of resource requirements given by users, and not the real needs of resources.*

DEFINITION 1.7.– Dynamic Scheduling – *Scheduling is said to be dynamic when tasks can be migrated from one worker node to another while they are processed; dynamic scheduling takes account of the real needs of resources.*

Scheduling is designed to meet one or more goals. Some goals are related to how fast tasks are processed. Others aim to distribute resources across tasks in a fair way. Others are intended for optimal use of resources, for example to balance the workload between resources, or to consolidate it on a few resources to maximize their utilization rate. Others are designed to enforce placement constraints, which can result from affinities or antagonisms between tasks. Finally, some goals may consist of enforcing other kinds of constraints, like precedence constraints.

Scheduling can take account of the volatility of the infrastructure, which results from the addition or removal of resources. This addition or removal may be wanted, if infrastructure owners desire to make more resources available to users, retire obsolete resources, or perform a maintenance operation on some resources (for example to update applications or replace faulty components). The removal can also be unwanted in case of hardware or software faults, which is more likely to happen if the infrastructure is large.

1.2.4. *Deployment of tasks*

Once the scheduler has decided which resources to assign to a task, it needs to deploy the latter on the right worker node.

This may require installing and configuring an appropriate runtime, in addition to the copy of programs and data necessary to process the task.

Data associated with the task can be stored: (1) locally on the worker node or (2) remotely, on a shared storage server, on a set of nodes hosting a distributed file system, or in a storage array.

1.2.5. *Monitoring the infrastructure*

Each task is likely to be migrated from one worker node to another if dynamic scheduling is applied; in this case, the scheduler uses information collected by the monitoring system; monitoring is also interesting for other purposes.

Monitoring enables system administrators to obtain information on the state of the infrastructure, and especially to be notified in case of hardware or software faults.

Monitoring can also be used to take account of the resource consumption of each user to ensure that everyone complies with the terms of use of the infrastructure.

Finally, monitoring enables users to know the state of their tasks: waiting to be processed, being processed or terminated.

1.2.6. *Termination of tasks*

Once their tasks are terminated, users should be able to retrieve the results.

After that, it may be necessary to clean the resources, to come back to a default configuration, so that they can be used to process other tasks.

1.3. Frameworks traditionally used to manage distributed infrastructures

The concepts presented in the previous section have been implemented in the frameworks that are traditionally used to manage distributed infrastructures. Some of them are frameworks implemented in user space [FOS 06, LAU 06], while others are distributed operating systems [MUL 90, PIK 95, LOT 05, RIL 06, COR 08].

1.3.1. *User-space frameworks*

User-space frameworks are highly popular in managing distributed infrastructures.

DEFINITION 1.8.– User-space Framework – *A user-space framework is a piece of software built on an existing operating system.*

The user-space frameworks providing the most functionalities, like Globus [FOS 06] or gLite [LAU 06], are able to manage grids; incidentally, gLite was originally designed to manage EGEE, the ex-European grid, which has been mentioned previously.

These user-space frameworks rely on batch schedulers; the latter can intrinsically be part of the former, or exist as independent projects, like Condor [THA 05], Torque/PBS [ADA 12] or OAR [CAP 05]. Batch schedulers aim to maximize the utilization rate of the resources. They commonly perform static scheduling, and follow a centralized or hierarchical approach (the scheduler runs on a single node or on a few nodes organized in a hierarchical way, respectively).

1.3.2. Distributed operating systems

Distributed operating systems (DOSs) are an alternative to manage distributed infrastructures.

DEFINITION 1.9.– Distributed Operating System – *A distributed operating system (DOS) is designed to integrate the functionalities related to distributed infrastructures inside the operating system, to improve performance and simplicity of use [COR 08]. It may be designed from scratch, or from an existing (non-distributed) operating system that has been heavily modified.*

Some DOSs are designed more specifically to build single system images.

DEFINITION 1.10.– Single System Image – *A single system image is "the property of a system that hides the heterogeneous and distributed nature of the available resources and presents them to users and applications as a single unified computing resource" [BUY 01].*

There are many DOSs, including Amoeba [MUL 90], Plan 9 [PIK 95], OpenMosix [LOT 05], OpenSSI [LOT 05], Kerrighed [LOT 05], Vigne [RIL 06] and XtreemOS [COR 08]. Some DOSs are dedicated to grids (like Vigne and XtreemOS), others to clusters (such as Amoeba, Plan 9, Mosix, OpenSSI and Kerrighed). It is worth noting that a DOS for grids may be built on a DOS for clusters, like XtreemOS with Kerrighed.

Several DOSs for clusters (in particular, Mosix, OpenSSI and Kerrighed) dynamically schedule tasks, in a more decentralized way than batch schedulers, given that the scheduling work is distributed across all worker nodes. Mosix, OpenSSI and Kerrighed try, by default, to balance the workload of central processing units. However, these DOSs are unable to migrate some kinds of tasks, especially those that highly depend on the resources of the worker nodes, where they were initially placed; for example, they need to have direct access to graphics or network cards.

The development of DOSs was gradually abandoned, especially because they are complex to maintain and update. This led people to opt not only for the user-space frameworks, mentioned previously, but also for new user-space frameworks that target virtual infrastructures.

1.4. Conclusion

In this chapter, we presented the main categories of distributed infrastructures that exist nowadays: clusters, data centers, grids and volunteer computing platforms.

Then, we identified the main functionalities provided by most of the distributed infrastructure managers: secured connection of users to the infrastructure, submission of tasks, their scheduling, their deployment on the resources they were assigned to, their monitoring and their termination.

Finally, we described the managers that are traditionally used on these infrastructures: user-space frameworks and DOSs.

In the next chapter, we will see how virtualization has revolutionized the management and use of distributed infrastructures to give birth to a new computing paradigm: cloud computing.

2

Contributions of Virtualization

Virtualization [SMI 05] enables us to (1) dissociate high-level software layers from the low-level ones and/or from the hardware to (2) dupe the former regarding the real characteristics of the latter.

Virtualization has been used since the 60s [CRE 81]. The hardware prerequisites for its use have been formally stated in the 70s [POP 74]. Over the past few years, virtualization has been increasingly used on distributed infrastructures due to its advantages in terms of management and utilization of resources.

In this chapter, we introduce the main concepts related to virtualization, and we focus on its contributions with regard to the management and utilization of resources in distributed infrastructures, contributions that have led to the rise of cloud computing.

2.1. Introduction to virtualization

2.1.1. *System and application virtualization*

Virtualization is presented in two main categories [SMI 05]: system virtualization and application virtualization.

2.1.1.1. *System virtualization*

System virtualization aims at virtualizing only the hardware.

DEFINITION 2.1.– System virtual machine (in the strict sense) – *A system virtual machine is a piece of software equivalent to a given physical machine, that is to say an aggregation of processing units, memory and devices (hard disk drive, network card, graphics card, etc.).*

To use a system virtual machine, it is necessary to install applications and an operating software; the latter is called a guest operating system, to shed light on the fact that it is not installed on a physical machine (see Figure 2.1).

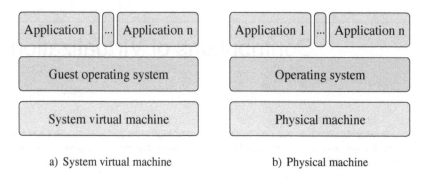

a) System virtual machine   b) Physical machine

Figure 2.1. *Comparison between a system virtual machine and a physical machine*

DEFINITION 2.2.– System virtual machine (in the broad sense) – *The expression* system virtual machine *is commonly used to refer to the virtual machine in the strict sense, but also to the guest operating system and the applications it hosts.*

Virtual machines are hosted by physical machines, on which a hypervisor is installed.

DEFINITION 2.3.– Hypervisor – *A hypervisor is a piece of software in charge of (1) assigning resources from one or several physical machines to virtual machines and of (2) managing the virtual machines.*

Hypervisors can be grouped into two categories: native (or type I) hypervisors and hosted (or type II) hypervisors.

DEFINITION 2.4.– Native – or type I – hypervisor – *A native (or type I) hypervisor is "the only software that executes in the highest privilege level defined by the system architecture" [SMI 05].*

DEFINITION 2.5.– Hosted – or type II – hypervisor – *A hosted (or type II) hypervisor runs "on a host platform that is already running an existing OS" and "utilizes the functions already available on the host OS to control and manage resources desired by each of the virtual machines" [SMI 05]. A hosted hypervisor can either run entirely in the highest level of privilege, or run partially or completely in a less privileged mode.*

VMware ESX [WAL 02], Citrix XenServer [CIT 12] and Microsoft Hyper-V [CER 09] are examples of native hypervisors, whereas Red Hat KVM (Kernel-based virtual machine) [KIV 07] is a hosted hypervisor.

2.1.1.2. *Application virtualization*

Contrary to system virtualization, application virtualization does not virtualize only the hardware.

DEFINITION 2.6.– Application virtual machine – *An application virtual machine is a software equivalent of a physical machine and part or the totality of an operating system.*

Using an application virtual machine necessitates installing applications and the fraction of the operating system that is not virtualized (see Figure 2.2).

Similarly to system virtual machines, application virtual machines are hosted on physical machines. However, instead of being managed by a hypervisor, they are administered by the operating system.

The two most famous implementations of application virtualization are:

– Containers [SOL 07, BHA 08], which are generally used to partition the resources of the underlying physical machine; each container can run several applications;

– High-level language virtual machines, like the Java virtual machine (JVM) [LIN 99]; by means of application virtualization, a given Java program can run on every operating system with a JVM;

however, contrary to a container, a JVM can only run a single Java program; to run several Java programs, it is necessary to start the corresponding number of JVMs.

In the following, we will focus on system virtualization.

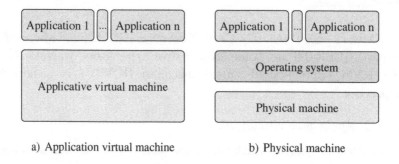

a) Application virtual machine   b) Physical machine

Figure 2.2. *Comparison between an application virtual machine and a physical machine*

2.1.2. *Abstractions created by hypervisors*

System virtualization enables a hypervisor to dupe the software installed on a virtual machine regarding the real characteristics of the underlying physical resources. These resources can be abstracted in three ways by the hypervisor: translation; aggregation of resources; or partition of resources.

2.1.2.1. *Translation*

If the processor of the physical machine and the one of the virtual machine do not belong to the same architecture, the hypervisor has to translate the instructions executed by the virtual machine (on behalf of the guest operating system and the applications it hosts) into instructions that can be executed by the physical machine (see Figure 2.3(a)) [BEL 05].

2.1.2.2. *Aggregation of resources*

A hypervisor aggregates resources if it enables a guest operating system and applications to run on several physical machines, by giving them the illusion of a single, big machine (see Figure 2.3(b)) [CHA 09].

2.1.2.3. *Partition of resources*

On the contrary, a hypervisor partitions resources if it enables a given physical machine to host several virtual machines (see Figure 2.3(c)) [WAL 02, BAR 03, KIV 07, CER 09].

In the following, we will focus on resource partitioning.

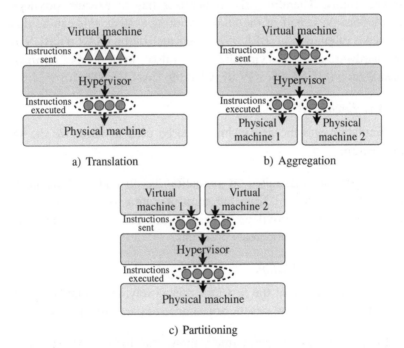

Figure 2.3. *Abstractions created by hypervisors*

2.1.3. *Virtualization techniques used by hypervisors*

Hypervisors can rely on several virtualization techniques to make a guest operating system run on a system virtual machine.

It can be a challenge to fulfill this objective, depending on the architecture of the processor of the underlying physical machine, since this architecture does not necessarily meet the prerequisites identified by Popek and Goldberg [POP 74] to be easily virtualized. The x86 architecture, which is the most common one on computers nowadays, is thus hard to virtualize [ROB 00].

To understand the root of this problem, it is worth knowing that an operating system is used to having full power on the underlying physical machine; in other words, it can execute whatever instruction it needs. However, in the context of system virtualization, this full power is given to the hypervisor; the guest operating system is granted only limited rights. Therefore, the hypervisor has to execute privileged instructions on behalf of the guest operating system; this can be done by means of emulation [BEL 05], paravirtualization [BAR 03, RUS 07] or hardware-assisted virtualization (also known as *hardware virtualization*) [UHL 05, KIV 07, CER 09, LAN 10, STE 10].

2.1.3.1. *Emulation*

Emulation was the first technique to be used to virtualize the x86 architecture.

A hypervisor that relies on emulation has to replace dynamically the instructions coming from the guest operating system (that require the highest level of privilege to be executed correctly) by equivalent instructions that will not create problems.

2.1.3.2. *Paravirtualization*

The performance of the first hypervisors relying on emulation was not optimal, which explains the appearance of paravirtualization.

In the context of paravirtualization, the hypervisor exposes a specific interface to the guest operating system, to let the latter execute privileged instructions correctly.

The guest operating system has to be modified to use the new interface, which is a time-consuming and complex operation. Such a modified operating system is said to be *paravirtualized*.

2.1.3.3. *Hardware virtualization*

Given the popularity of virtualization, the designers of x86 processors finally decided to create hardware extensions to ease the development of new hypervisors.

These extensions are in charge of executing privileged instructions on behalf of the guest operating system, without necessitating modifications or emulation.

It is worth noting that hypervisors have been more and more likely to combine the three virtualization techniques presented in this section. Hardware virtualization has been commonly used by recent hypervisors to virtualize the processor and the memory, since it is the easiest technique to implement [KIV 07, CER 09, LAN 10, STE 10]. Regarding device virtualization, hypervisors generally let the user choose between emulation and paravirtualization, the latter providing better performance [NUS 09].

2.1.4. *Main functionalities provided by hypervisors*

Hypervisors provide several functionalities. In this section, we focus on those that are most interesting to manage resources in a distributed infrastructure.

2.1.4.1. *Resource throttling*

A hypervisor can provide several possibilities to limit virtual machine resource consumption, for example, to guarantee a fair share of resources.

Xen especially authorizes assigning a weight to a given virtual machine; the latter is then granted access to the processor for a duration that is proportional to its weight [CHI 07].

Moreover, a type II hypervisor relying on Linux as the host operating system can make use of cgroups [MEN 13, PRP 13]. The main idea is to assign one or more virtual machines to a given cgroup.

Regarding the processor, it is possible to assign a weight to each cgroup; a cgroup with a weight equal to 2 can, therefore, use twice as much processor as a cgroup with a weight equal to 1 unit. Furthermore, on a physical machine that has multiple processors, cgroups allow us to specify which processors can be used by a given cgroup.

Concerning the memory, it is possible to limit the amount used or the slots of memory a given cgroup can have access to.

With respect to the network, cgroups allow us to assign a weight to each network interface, to restrict the outgoing network traffic.

Finally, in the case of block devices, it is possible to assign a weight to a given cgroup, to give it corresponding access to all devices or to a given device. It is also feasible to limit the number of read or write operations, as well as the amount of data transferred during reads and writes.

2.1.4.2. *Optimizing memory usage*

The functionalities presented so far exclusively aimed at restricting virtual machines' use of resources, without trying to optimize it. Optimizing memory usage is a good way to (1) avoid a starvation that would have an impact on the performance of virtual machines and to (2) start more virtual machines on a given physical one.

One of the first optimizations consists of letting the hypervisor retrieve control on the slots (*pages*) of memory that are not used by the virtual machines; this is done by means of *ballooning* [WAL 02]. When the hypervisor wants to recall pages from a guest operating system, it instructs a *balloon* application which is loaded into the guest operating system to inflate. The guest operating system then allocates memory to the balloon application. The balloon application tells the hypervisor which pages it owns, in other words which pages have been freed. Finally, the hypervisor can use the freed pages. This process is reversible: the hypervisor can give the pages back to the guest operating system if needed.

Another optimization lies in *memory deduplication* [WAL 02, ARC 09], which works as follows: the hypervisor scans the content of memory pages owned by each virtual machine; when it finds two identical pages, it keeps only one copy and reuses the replicas for another purpose.

2.1.4.3. *Suspending and resuming virtual machines*

In addition to managing resources assigned to virtual machines, a hypervisor can also suspend a virtual machine and resume it later.

The state of the virtual machine can be either kept in memory or stored on the hard disk drive [PAR 11]. The latter option is particularly interesting, since it enables the hypervisor to (1) free the memory allocated to the virtual machine and to (2) resume the virtual machine even if the physical machine was rebooted, following, for example, a maintenance operation.

2.1.4.4. *Snapshotting*

Snapshotting is similar to the previous functionality. The main difference is that the state of the virtual machine disk is saved, in addition to the state of the processor and the memory.

Several snapshots can be stored, each one corresponding to a different moment in the life of the virtual machine.

It is then possible to "travel through time into the past" and restore the state of the virtual machine at the time the snapshot was taken. Snapshotting is especially interesting to bring the virtual machine back to a viable state, following its corruption.

2.1.4.5. *Migrating virtual machines*

Finally, migration is a key functionality to manage virtual machines in distributed infrastructures. Migrating a virtual machine consists of moving it from the source physical machine to a destination virtual machine. Migration can be used to transfer the workload from a physical machine to another one, or to free a physical machine from its virtual machines, to perform a maintenance operation.

Migration exists in two flavors: *cold* and *live* migration [CLA 05]. Cold migration consists of (1) suspending the virtual machine,

(2) transferring its state on the destination physical machine and (3) resuming the virtual machine. Alternatively, live migration aims at minimizing the time during which the virtual machine is inactive; to reach this objective, most of the state of the virtual machine is transferred while it is active.

Migrating a virtual machine is a costly operation, since it consumes processor and network resources [CLA 05, HER 10]. Moreover, the virtual machine should always have access to its virtual hard disk drive; this objective can be achieved by storing the virtual hard disk drive on a storage space that is accessible by the source physical machine as well as the destination one; otherwise, if the virtual hard disk drive is stored locally on the source physical machine, it has to be transferred on the destination one when the virtual machine is migrating, which is more expensive.

2.2. Virtualization and management of distributed infrastructures

Virtualization is commonly used in distributed infrastructures, given its advantages for the owners as well as the users of these infrastructures [FOS 08, VOG 08, ERI 09, HER 09, LOW 09].

2.2.1. *Contributions of virtualization to the management of distributed infrastructures*

2.2.1.1. *Advantages for owners*

2.2.1.1.1. Improving resource sharing

Virtualization first enables owners to improve resource sharing among users by hosting virtual machines belonging to different users on the same nodes. This is made possible by resource throttling mechanisms (like those provided by the cgroups), to finely assign resources to virtual machines, and by the relative strong isolation between virtual machines hosted on the same node (in theory, a virtual machine cannot get access to the state and the data of another virtual machine).

Resource usage can be optimized by (1) leveraging functionalities provided by hypervisors (like ballooning or memory deduplication), or by (2) migrating virtual machines to take account of the workload fluctuations (to balance the workload or to consolidate it).

Consolidation enables owners to use fewer nodes, which implies a less powerful cooling system. Consequently, the power consumption decreases (since there are fewer nodes to power and cool), as well as the financial cost.

2.2.1.1.2. Facilitating maintenance operations

Moreover, virtualization facilitates maintenance operations. If system administrators want to perform a maintenance operation on a subset of the infrastructure, they only have to move the impacted virtual machines somewhere else; the maintenance operation is, therefore, completely transparent for users.

Deploying a minimal runtime. Finally, virtualization enables system administrators to deploy a minimal runtime on each node, without requiring customization to match user needs. Users are indeed in charge of setting their own runtime.

2.2.1.2. *Advantages for users*

2.2.1.2.1. Deploying a customized runtime

Users are in charge of customizing and providing their own runtime. They can install the guest operating system and the applications they want on their virtual machines. They are not limited to the runtime of the distributed infrastructure.

2.2.1.2.2. Outsourcing infrastructure buy and management

Users do not have to build their own infrastructure; they can outsource its buy and management, and therefore avoid this complex and costly operation.

Even better, they are not limited by an infrastructure that can hardly evolve. They can use more or fewer resources on the virtual infrastructure, according to their real needs, which can change. For instance, the workload of an Intranet website will be higher during working hours.

2.2.1.2.3. Fault-tolerance and high availability

Finally, some infrastructures provide users with fault-tolerance and high availability features. Fault-tolerance functionalities guarantee users against loosing their data, if faults occur on the infrastructure. Regarding high availability, it ensures that virtual machines will be restored as quickly as possible, so that they are almost always available.

2.2.2. *Virtualization and cloud computing*

Virtualization has contributed to the rise of cloud computing, given its usefulness in distributed infrastructures.

DEFINITION 2.7.– Cloud computing – *Cloud computing is "a large-scale distributed computing paradigm that is driven by economies of scale, in which a pool of abstracted, virtualized, dynamically-scalable, managed computing power, storage, platforms, and services are delivered on demand to external customers over the Internet" [FOS 08].*

Virtualization is particularly used for infrastructure as a service (IaaS), which aims to provide users with raw virtual machines, and letting them install the guest operating system and the applications they want.

IaaS can be used as a building block for higher-level types of cloud computing, such as platform as a service (PaaS) or software as a service (SaaS) (see Figure 2.4). PaaS provides users with a development environment, to let them develop and deploy their own applications. Alternatively, SaaS consists of hosting one or more applications that can be used directly, such as on-line mailing systems or office suites.

Amazon Web Services [AWS 13], Google App Engine [GAE 13], Microsoft Windows Azure [AZU 13], Force.com [FOR 13] and

Salesforce.com [SAL 13] are examples of cloud computing providers (see the time line on Figure 2.5).

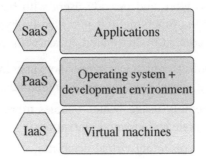

Figure 2.4. *Main categories of cloud computing*

Figure 2.5. *Order of appearance of some cloud computing services*

2.3. Conclusion

In this chapter, we presented the main concepts related to virtualization, as well as their utility in the context of distributed infrastructures.

We first defined what a virtual machine was and identified the differences between system and application virtual machines.

Then, we studied hypervisors, which are brokers between virtual machines and physical machines. We saw that they can abstract the hardware in three different ways, by translating instructions, aggregating resources or partitioning resources. We noticed that the most recent hypervisors tend to combine several virtualization techniques (emulation, paravirtualization and hardware virtualization) to ease developers' work and provide users with better performance. We also described the functionalities provided by hypervisors that are most useful in the context of distributed infrastructures, namely:

– resource throttling, which lets hypervisors guarantee a fair sharing of resources among virtual machines on a single node;

– optimizing memory usage, which enables more virtual machines to run on the same node and prevents starvation;

– suspending and resuming virtual machines;

– snapshotting virtual machines, to save their states and restore them later, if necessary;

– migrating virtual machines from one physical machine to another, to transfer the workload and facilitate maintenance operations.

We then focused on the advantages of using virtualization in distributed infrastructures. Virtualization enables infrastructure owners to improve resource sharing, perform maintenance operations more easily and deploy a minimal runtime. On the users' side, virtualization allows them to deploy a customized runtime that meets their needs, outsource the buy and management of the infrastructure and employ high availability and fault-tolerance features. We finally shed light on the fact that virtualization has contributed to the rise of cloud computing in general, and IaaS in particular.

In the next chapter, we will study the virtual infrastructure managers that are used in production.

3

Virtual Infrastructure Managers Used in Production

System virtualization has been commonly used over the past few years, due to its advantages for infrastructure owners as well as users.

This interest, which exists in academic as well as industrial communities, has led to the development of many software frameworks dedicated to the management of virtual infrastructures.

In this chapter, we study the main virtual infrastructure managers (VIMs) that are used in production. More specifically, we focus on their architecture, the main features they provide and their limitations.

3.1. Overview of virtual infrastructure managers

3.1.1. *Generalities*

VIMs are based on concepts that are very similar to those presented in Chapter 1. Like for a nonvirtual infrastructure, a user should be able to connect to the system, by means of an access node. Then, before being able to process tasks, he/she needs to create at least one virtual machine. To make this step easier and faster, the manager usually provides templates, in other words preconfigured virtual machines with a guest operating system, and a given capacity in processor, memory, hard disk drive and network. Once the template is chosen, the scheduler looks for free resources to create the virtual machine; the scheduler especially decides (1) which storage space to copy the virtual machine disk image to and (2) which worker node to start the virtual machine on.

3.1.2. *Classification*

VIMs can be grouped into several categories.

Some frameworks resulted from academic research, such as Eucalyptus [NUR 09, EUC 12] (created at the University of California and promoted by Eucalyptus Systems), Nimbus [NIM 13] (developed at the University of Chicago) and OpenNebula [SOT 09, OPE 13] (designed at the University of Madrid and supported by C12G Labs, with contributions from several partners). We call these managers *academic frameworks*.

Other managers were designed and have been developed by a single company, such as Microsoft System Center Virtual Machine Manager (SCVMM) [MIC 12], VMware vSphere [VMW 11] and vCloud [VMW 10] (vCloud adds features to vSphere) and Citrix XenServer [CIT 12]. We call these managers *proprietary frameworks*.

The remaining managers were designed by companies and have been supported by a community of developers, such as CloudStack [APA 12] (produced by Citrix) and OpenStack [OPE 12] (started by NASA and Rackspace). We call these managers *community frameworks*.

3.2. Resource organization

Like for traditional frameworks used to manage distributed infrastructures (see Chapter 1), VIMs are in charge of operating two main kinds of resources: computing and storage.

3.2.1. *Computing resources*

Even though the terms used differ greatly depending on the VIM considered, they tend to organize computing resources in a similar way.

3.2.1.1. *Computing nodes and supported hypervisors*

The computing unit is the node, and each node hosts a hypervisor.

Academic and community frameworks support several hypervisors: KVM, Xen (or derivative products such as XenServer or Xen Cloud Platform), ESX(i) and even Hyper-V in the case of OpenStack. Nimbus is the only exception, since it supports only KVM and Xen.

On the contrary, proprietary frameworks usually rely on the hypervisor designed by the same company. Thus, VMware vCloud and vSphere are based on ESXi, and the XenServer ecosystem is built on the eponym hypervisor. However, Microsoft SCVMM can use Hyper-V, as well as ESX or XenServer.

3.2.1.2. *Grouping unit*

The smallest grouping unit, which offers the most flexibility, is equivalent to an arbitrary number of nodes belonging to the same cluster. This unit is called *VMM pool* in Nimbus, *virtual datacenter* in OpenNebula (with the oZones extension), *host groups* in SCVMM and *resource pool* in vCloud/vSphere, XenServer and OpenStack.

The cluster is another grouping unit, which exists in Eucalyptus, OpenNebula and CloudStack.

3.2.1.3. *Sets of grouping units*

The smallest set of grouping units usually corresponds to a fraction of a data center. It is called *availability zone* in Nimbus and OpenStack, *private cloud* in SCVMM, *virtual datacenter* in vCloud and *pod* in CloudStack.

The biggest set of grouping units is called *zone*, and is typically a whole data center. This concept appears in OpenNebula (with the oZones extension) and CloudStack, and is currently under development for OpenStack. There are several opportunities linked to zone management: (1) provide users of two different zones with strong isolation, (2) decrease the latency by assigning users to the closest zone and (3) limit the consequences of failures impacting a whole site by providing a backup zone.

3.2.2. *Storage resources*

The organization of storage resources is similar to the one of computing resources.

3.2.2.1. *Local storage on worker nodes*

Some frameworks rely on local storage of worker nodes to keep part or the totality of virtual machine disk images. Relying on local storage guarantees high performance.

Nimbus stores the totality of virtual machine disk images on worker nodes. OpenNebula and CloudStack can be configured to do the same.

However, Eucalyptus and OpenStack only store root partitions on worker nodes, each root partition containing the guest operating system and most of the applications of a virtual machine.

3.2.2.2. *Shared storage*

Many frameworks rely on storage that is shared among the worker nodes of the same grouping unit; shared storage is a complement or a replacement to local storage. Shared storage can also be used to keep part or the totality of virtual machine disk images.

Eucalyptus and OpenStack store only persistent user data on a shared storage. Eucalyptus uses *storage controllers* (each one of them is associated with a *cluster*), whereas OpenStack leverages Cinder.

Other solutions that rely on shared storage use are to keep the totality of virtual machine disk images, as well as snapshots (excepting CloudStack, which stores snapshots elsewhere, as we will see later). Shared storage enables virtual machines to be live migrated between nodes connected to the same storage space. SCVMM uses *storage pools* (linked with *host groups*), vCloud/vSphere uses *datastores* (assigned to *resource pools*) and XenServer uses *storage repositories* (associated with *resource pools*). If OpenNebula and CloudStack are configured to use a shared storage, they use respectively *datastores* and *primary storages* in conjunction with *clusters*.

3.2.2.3. *Secondary storage*

In addition to local and/or shared storage, VIMs may use a secondary storage, associated with a set of grouping units, to store long-term data that do not require fast access, especially:

– snapshots, when they are not kept on a shared storage;

– virtual machine templates;

– other kinds of data.

Eucalyptus uses Walrus as a secondary storage, Nimbus uses Cumulus, OpenNabula uses a *template repository*, SCVMM a *VMM library*, vCloud uses specific *datastores*, XenServer uses particular *storage repositories*, CloudStack uses a *secondary storage* and OpenStack leverages Glance (for templates and snapshots) and Swift (for other kinds of data).

Information related to resource organization is summarized in Table 3.1.

3.3. Scheduling

The dispatching of virtual machines on physical resources, and more specifically on worker nodes, is done by dedicated schedulers, which we are going to study.

3.3.1. *Scheduler architecture*

The schedulers of the main VIMs used in production either follow a centralized or hierarchical architecture.

3.3.1.1. *Centralized architecture*

DEFINITION 3.1.– Centralized scheduler – *In the case of a centralized architecture, the scheduler is installed on a single node.*

The vast majority of the schedulers of the VIMs studied follow a centralized architecture (see Figure 3.1(a)). Only those of Eucalyptus and XenServer follow a hierarchical approach.

Name	Supported Hypervisors	Computing Resources	Storage Resources
Eucalyptus 3.1.1	*ESXi *KVM *Xen	Clusters (also called *availability zones*)	*Local (root partitions) *Storage controllers (persistent storage of VMs) *Walrus (templates, snapshots)
Nimbus 2.10	*KVM *Xen	*Vmm pools *Availability zones	*Local (disk images) *Cumulus (templates, snapshots)
OpenNebula 3.8	*ESX *KVM *Xen	*Clusters *Virtual data centers (1 VDC = fraction of a cluster) *Zones (1 *zone* = 1 data center)	*Local (disk images of running VMs, if they are copied to local storage when VMs are instantiated) *Local, on the frontend (disk images stopped VMs, if they are copied to local storage when VMs are instantiated) *Datastores (disk images, snapshots, ISO files) *Template repository
SCVMM 2012	*ESX *Hyper-V *XenServer	*Host groups *Private Clouds	*Storage pools (disk images, snapshots) *Vmm library (templates, ISO files)
vCloud / vSphere 5.1	ESXi	*Resource pools (1 RP = fraction of a cluster; max 32 nodes in a cluster) *vCloud provider virtual datacenters (1 PVDC = 1 vSphere cluster) *vCloud organization VDC (1 OVDC = fraction of a PVDC)	*Datastores (disk images, snapshots, ISO files, vCloud templates) *Storage of the user's machine or URL (vSphere template)
XenServer 6.0	XenServer	Resource pools (1 RP = fraction of a cluster; max 16 nodes in a cluster)	Storage repositories (disk images, snapshots, ISO files, templates)
CloudStack 4.0.0	*ESX *KVM *Xen, XenServer	*Clusters *Pods *Zones (typically a data center)	*Local (disk images, if configured like this) *Primary storage (cluster; disk images, if configured like this) *Secondary storage (zone; templates, ISO files and snapshots)
OpenStack Folsom	*ESXi *Hyper-V *KVM *Xen, XenServer, Xen Cloud Platform	*Resource pools *Availability zones *Zones (work in progress)	*Local (root partitions) *Cinder, formerly Nova volume workers (persistent storage of VMs) *Glance (templates, ISO files and snapshots) *Swift (other kinds of data)

Table 3.1. *Resource organization*

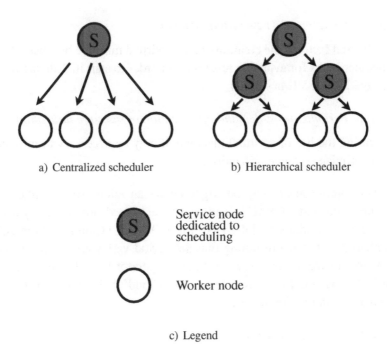

a) Centralized scheduler   b) Hierarchical scheduler

S   Service node
     dedicated to
     scheduling

○   Worker node

c) Legend

Figure 3.1. *Comparison between a centralized scheduler and a hierarchical one*

3.3.1.2. *Hierarchical architecture*

DEFINITION 3.2.– Hierarchical scheduler – *In the case of a hierarchical architecture, the scheduler is made up of several components that are organized in a hierarchical way. Each component is in charge of managing a subset of the infrastructure.*

The hierarchies implemented by Eucalyptus and XenServer have two echelons (see Figure 3.1(b)). The first one coincides with the scheduling at the *cluster* or *resource pool* level. The second one is related to the scheduling at the infrastructure level.

3.3.2. *Factors triggering scheduling*

Whatever the architecture is, several factors may trigger scheduling.

3.3.2.1. *Creation of a new virtual machine*

The first factor is the creation of a new virtual machine by a user. The scheduler looks for available resources, in order to start it. This factor is managed by all VIMs studied.

3.3.2.2. *Periodic or on-demand optimization of resource utilization*

During the life of a virtual machine, it may be necessary to migrate it, to optimize resource utilization.

This optimization may be triggered by an administrator (like for OpenNebula and SCVMM) and/or be performed automatically and periodically by the scheduler (like for SCVMM, vCloud/vSphere and XenServer). It is worth noting that the period varies greatly from one VIM to another: it can be set by an administrator from 10 min to 24 h for SCVMM, and from 1 min to 1 h for vCloud/vSphere; however, it is fixed to 2 min for XenServer.

3.3.2.3. *Node maintenance*

At another moment during the life of a virtual machine, an administrator may need to perform a maintenance operation on the node that hosts this virtual machine, for instance to update software or change a faulty physical component.

To avoid negative impacts on the virtual machine, the administrator can either (1) shut it down during the maintenance or (2) migrate it to another node. This evacuation process may be done automatically by the scheduler, like for OpenNebula, SCVMM, vCloud/vSphere, XenServer and CloudStack.

3.3.2.4. *Virtual machine crash*

Finally, a virtual machine can crash, due to software or hardware faults. In case, the virtual machine has to be highly available, the scheduler is notified and can then restart it.

This feature is proposed by OpenNebula, SCVMM, vCloud/vSphere, XenServer and CloudStack. It is also under development for OpenStack.

3.3.3. *Scheduling policies*

Once scheduling is started, it applies a given scheduling policy, which defines which resources to assign in priority to a given set of virtual machines.

All VIMs studied in this chapter propose their own scheduling policies. Only Nimbus is able to use an external batch scheduler to manage resources.

3.3.3.1. *First fit*

The first fit policy is the simplest one, since it aims to select the first node with enough free resources to host the newly created virtual machine.

This policy is implemented by Eucalyptus and CloudStack.

3.3.3.2. *Random*

Another approach, which is derived from the first fit policy, consists of listing all nodes that can host the new virtual machine, and choosing one of them randomly.

This approach is proposed by OpenStack.

3.3.3.3. *Load balancing*

Instead of selecting a node randomly, it may be more interesting to try to balance the workload among all nodes, so that the virtual machines can get the best performance. In this case, the less loaded nodes are used in priority to host virtual machines.

The workload can be defined in several ways, especially depending on:

– the number of virtual machines hosted on a node; OpenNebula *striping* algorithm is based on this definition;

– the memory utilization of a node; Nimbus *round robin* algorithm and OpenStack *filter* scheduler (when it is configured to perform load balancing) use this definition;

– the processor utilization of a node; OpenNebula *load-aware* algorithm is built on this definition;

– a combination of several resources utilization rates of a node, for instance (1) processor and memory in the case of vSphere *distributed resource scheduling* algorithm or (2) processor, memory, hard disk drive and network in the case of SCVMM *dynamic optimization* and XenServer *performance* algorithms.

3.3.3.4. *Consolidation*

Contrary to load balancing, consolidation aims at maximizing resource utilization on a restricted number of nodes.

As for load balancing, a consolidation algorithm can take account of several criteria:

– the number of virtual machines hosted on a node; the OpenNebula *packing* algorithm does so;

– the memory utilization of a node; this is used by the Nimbus *greedy* algorithm and OpenStack *filter* scheduler (when it is configured to perform consolidation);

– a combination of several resource utilization rates of a node, such as (1) processor and memory for vSphere *distributed power management* or (2) processor, memory, hard disk drive and network for SCVMM *power optimization* and XenServer *density* algorithms.

A dynamic consolidation algorithm can be used to free some nodes of all their virtual machines. These nodes can then be shut down, to save energy. They are booted only when they are necessary to host virtual machines. This feature is provided by SCVMM, vSphere and XenServer.

3.3.3.5. *Affinities and antagonisms*

Finally, another scheduling policy, which can be used in complement to one of the aforementioned policies, is based on the specification of affinities and antagonisms.

These affinities and antagonisms may be specified either (1) between virtual machines or (2) between a group of virtual machines on the one hand, and a group of nodes on the other hand.

In case affinities/antagonisms are specified between virtual machines, the objective is to:

– group on the same node the virtual machines that have affinities between them (for instance to let them communicate more rapidly);

– prevent two antagonist virtual machines from being hosted on the same node (for example, to avoid all virtual machines related to a website crashing simultaneously).

In case affinities/antagonisms are specified between a group of virtual machines and a group of nodes, the goal is to:

– favor, or even force, the placement of virtual machines on the nodes they have affinities for;

– forbid the placement of virtual machines on nodes they have antagonisms toward.

All of these kinds of affinities/antagonisms are available in vSphere. Moreover, OpenStack provides affinities/antagonisms between virtual machines only.

Information related to scheduling is summarized in Table 3.2.

3.4. Advantages

In addition to virtual machine scheduling, the VIMs studied in this chapter have several advantages, for infrastructure owners as well as users. We will focus on interfaces, isolation between users, scalability and high availability.

Name	Kind of Scheduling	Scheduling Triggering	Scheduling Policies	Resources Considered for Scheduling
Eucalyptus 3.1.1	Static	Creation of a VM	First fit	-
Nimbus 2.10	Static	Creation of a VM	*Nimbus (*greedy* = memory consolidation; *round robin* = memory load balancing) *Local Resource Manager (e.g., Torque)	Memory
OpenNebula 3.8	Static (mostly)	*Creation of a VM *On-demand rescheduling of a VM *Maintenance *Crash of a VM	*Packing*: Chooses the nodes with the most VMs *Striping*: Chooses the nodes with the least VMs *Load-aware*: processor load balancing	None or processor
SCVMM 2012	Dynamic	*Creation of a VM *Period (10 min $\leq$ period $\leq$ 24 h) *On-demand, on a *host group* *Maintenance *Crash of a VM	*Dynamic optimization* (load balancing) *Power optimization* (consolidation with node shutdown; optional feature of *dyn. optim.*)	*Processor *Memory *Hard disk drive (I/O) *Network (I/O)
vCloud / vSphere 5.1	Dynamic	*Creation of a VM *Period (1 min $\leq$ period $\leq$ 1 h, 5 minutes by default) *Maintenance *Crash of a VM	*Distributed resource scheduling* (load balancing) *Distributed power management* (consolidation with node shutdown) *Affinities and antagonisms (between VMs, or between of group of VMs and a group of nodes)	*Processor *Memory
XenServer 6.0	Dynamic	*Creation of a VM *Period (2 minutes) *Maintenance *Crash of a VM	*Performance* (load balancing) *Density* (consolidation with node shutdown)	*Processor *Memory *Hard disk drive (I/O) *Network (I/O)
CloudStack 4.0.0	Static (mostly)	*Creation of a VM *Maintenance *Crash of a VM	First fit	-
OpenStack Folsom	Static	*Creation of a VM	*Filter* : Chooses the node with the best score (in practice, memory load balancing or consolidation) *Chance*: Chooses a node randomly (with enough free resources) *Simple* (load balancing): chooses the least loaded node *Affinities and antagonisms (between VMs)	Memory

Table 3.2. *Virtual machine scheduling*

3.4.1. *Application programming interfaces and user interfaces*

The features provided by each VIM can be accessed by means of one or several application programming interfaces (APIs). It is worth noting that academic and community frameworks are partially compatible with the API of Amazon Elastic Compute Cloud (EC2). Thus, users can transfer their virtual machines onto a private infrastructure and still use the same tools. On the contrary, users can test the main features of EC2 on their own infrastructure before joining EC2. Recall that the EC2 API is a *de facto* standard, given the importance of Amazon in the Infrastructure as a Service market.

Tools to access to EC2, or to another virtual infrastructure, may be used in command line.

However, to make the use of virtual infrastructures easier for noncomputer specialists, they can also be accessed by means of graphical interfaces. These interfaces are commonly implemented as a web portal (like for all VIMs studied here), but sometimes also as a rich client (in other words, an application installed on the computer of the user).

3.4.2. *Isolation between users*

The features and resources a user can have access to may depend on the rights he/she has.

3.4.2.1. *Groups and quotas*

Users can be organized into groups.

Depending on the VIM used, it is then possible to specify, for a given group or user, which nodes can be used to create virtual machines on, how many virtual machines can be created and how much processor/memory/hard disk drive/network can be used.

These quotas enable infrastructure owners to protect users, by preventing a single user or a group of users from using too many resources.

3.4.2.2. *Network isolation*

Another way to protect users from one another consists of isolating the network traffic coming into or going out of virtual machines. The VIMs studied in this chapter provide two ways to fulfil this objective.

The first one is to configure virtual local area networks (VLAN), to isolate network traffics; each VLAN is virtually equivalent to a dedicated physical network. However, VLANs are not sufficient to isolate virtual machines that are connected to the Internet, since the network traffic going out of one VLAN can pass through the Internet before coming in another VLAN.

Network traffic filtering mitigates the limits of VLANs. The goal is to prevent some kinds of network traffic from coming in (or going out of) a virtual machine or a group of virtual machines. Eucalyptus, OpenNebula and OpenStack only allow filtering inbound traffic; on the contrary, vCloud/vSphere (*via* vShield Zones), XenServer (*via* Distributed vSwitch) and CloudStack allow to filter inbound as well as outbound traffics.

Information related to interfaces and network isolation is summarized in Table 3.3.

3.4.3. *Scalability*

Network configuration is a key operation. It does not only reinforce isolation between users, but also helps their applications to scale up. An application being able to scale up can bear an increase in workload without notably degrading the quality of service.

3.4.3.1. *Network load balancing*

One of the first ways of improving scalability, when a high traffic website is involved, consists of deploying this site on a group of virtual machines and in balancing the network traffic among them.

Name	Interfaces		Isolation	
	Support of EC2 API	Self Service Web Portal	VLAN	VM Network Traffic Filtering
Eucalyptus 3.1.1	Yes	Yes	Yes	*Inbound traffic *For a group of VMs (security group)
Nimbus 2.10	Yes	Yes	?	?
OpenNebula 3.8	Yes	Yes	Yes	*Black and white lists of ports, inbound traffic *For each VM created from a template specifying these lists
SCVMM 2012	No	Yes	Yes	?
vCloud / vSphere 5.1	No	Yes	Yes	*Inbound and outbound traffic *For all VMs in a data centre, a cluster or a network *Via vShield Zones
XenServer 6.0	No	Yes	Yes	*Inbound and outbound traffic *For a single VM, all VMs in a network, a pool or a data centre *Via Distributed vSwitch
CloudStack 4.0.0	Yes	Yes	Yes	*Inbound and outbound traffic *For a group of VMs (security group)
OpenStack Folsom	Yes	Yes	Yes	*Inbound traffic *For a group of VMs (security group)

Table 3.3. *Interfaces and network isolation*

The VIMs studied in this chapter implement several network load balancing policies:

– the round robin policy assigns each new connection (to the website) to a different virtual machine in the group; it is implemented by SCVMM, vCloud/vSphere, CloudStack and OpenStack;

– the least connection policy steers every new connection to the virtual machine that has the least connections to manage; it is provided by CloudStack and OpenStack;

– the source IP or hash IP policy directs every new connection to a given virtual machine, depending on the IP address this connection comes from; it is proposed by vCloud/vSphere and CloudStack.

3.4.3.2. *Auto scaling*

Network load balancing is particularly interesting when it is combined with application auto scaling. In other words, it is interesting when the VIM is able to start or shut down virtual machines hosting a given application, depending on the workload at a given moment.

This feature is provided by Nimbus, but only for the FutureGrid grid users. Moreover, it is under development for CloudStack and OpenStack.

3.4.4. *High availability and fault-tolerance*

The advantages described so far would be of limited interest if the VIM or the virtual machines crashed in cases of hardware faults. Fortunately, most of the VIMs studied in this chapter provide several mechanisms to mitigate the consequences of hardware faults. More specifically, the VIMs rely on service replication and automatic restarting.

3.4.4.1. *Definitions*

Replication allows restoring a service almost immediately in the case of crash, while minimizing data loss. Typically, a backup service is kept ready to take over from the main service; when a crash of the main service is detected, the backup service is activated.

Restarting a service automatically allows us to restore it rapidly, but less than replication. When a service crashes, it is restarted, potentially on a different node; however, it is necessary to wait during the whole initialization step before the service can be used again.

3.4.4.2. *High availability and fault-tolerance for virtual machines*

Virtual machine replication is proposed only by vCloud/vSphere. A "mirror" virtual machine is created on a node that is different from the one hosting the original virtual machine (that has to be marked as "highly available"); each operation performed on the original virtual machine is replicated on the mirror one; if the original machine crashes, the mirror one immediately takes over.

However, the virtual machine automatic restarting feature is provided by all VIMs studied in this chapter, with the exception of Eucalyptus and OpenStack (it is under development for the latter). In case a virtual machine marked as "highly available" crashes, it is automatically restarted, possibly on another node if the original one is down. To use this functionality, the virtual machine disk image has generally to be kept in a shared storage space that the source and destination nodes have access to.

3.4.4.3. *High availability and fault-tolerance for the virtual infrastructure manager*

Virtual machine high availability features are interesting, not only for the users, but also for some components of the VIM, if they are installed on virtual machines. Regarding the other components, it is necessary to decide on a case-by-case basis.

Databases have to be replicated, either by means of a built-in mechanism (like for MySQL and Oracle), or with an external mechanism (for instance, VMware vCenter Server Heartbeat for Microsoft SQL databases).

Finally, stateless components (in other words, those that can be restarted without data loss) can be either replicated or restarted automatically.

3.4.4.4. *Disaster recovery*

High availability features described so far are unfortunately useless in the case of disaster affecting a whole data center, such as long power cuts, storms, fires, floods, earthquakes or even plane crashes.

Nevertheless, some VIMs, such as vSphere and XenServer, can make disaster recovery easier by replicating data on a backup site.

Information related to scalability, high availability and fault-tolerance is summarized in Table 3.4.

Name	Scalability		High Availability		
	Network Load-balancing Between VMs	Application Auto Scaling	High Availability For VMs	High Availability for VIM Components	Disaster Recovery
Eucalyptus 3.1.1	No	No	No	Yes	?
Nimbus 2.10	?	Available for FutureGrid users *via* Phantom 0.1	Available for FutureGrid users *via* Phantom 0.1	?	?
OpenNebula 3.8	No	No	Yes	*MySQL replication *Front-end*: to be done manually	?
SCVMM 2012	Round robin	No	Yes	Yes	?
vCloud / vSphere 5.1	*Round robin *Hash IP (*via* vShield Edge Web LB, port 80 only)	?	Yes	*vCenter Server: *via* vCenter Server Heartbeat *vCenter DB: *via* Heartbeat (if MS SQL) or Oracle RAC (if Oracle) *Other DBs: Oracle RAC *vCenter Chargeback: necessary to spread components *vCloud Director: deployed as a pool of HA VMs	Yes (*via* vCenter Site Recovery Manager)
XenServer 6.0	?	?	Yes	*Pool master*	Yes
CloudStack 4.0.0	*Round robin *Least connection *Source IP	Under development	Yes	Yes *Supports multiple management servers *MySQL replication	No
OpenStack Folsom	(*Via* Atlas LB) *Round robin *Least connection	Scheduled, *via* Heat	Scheduled, *via* Heat	?	?

Table 3.4. *Scalability and high availability*

3.5. Limits

Even though the VIMs studied in this chapter have a lot of advantages, they also have drawbacks, especially regarding schedulers and interfaces.

3.5.1. *Scheduling*

First, half of the VIMs studied in this chapter cannot optimize resource utilization dynamically. Given that the workload of a virtual machine can fluctuate from one moment to another, it would not necessarily consume all resources its node provides it with. Definitively, it means that some resources would be underutilized.

Then, the reactivity of schedulers providing dynamic optimization is perfectible. It is thus necessary to wait for up to 2 min with XenServer, 5 min with vSphere (it is possible to decrease this time to 1 min, but it is not recommended by VMware) and even 10 min with SCVMM before an overloaded node problem is detected, without even taking account of the time to solve this problem. In other words, the quality of service can be degraded for a given amount of time.

Moreover, rescheduling virtual machines in cases of maintenance or crash should be available in all VIMs, respectively to facilitate administrators' work and to improve user application availability.

Furthermore, the VIMs studied in this chapter (with the exception of vSphere) need a shared storage to migrate virtual machines from one node to another. Unfortunately, this shared storage can become a bottleneck if several virtual machines simultaneously perform many read/write operations on their respective disk images [KOT 10]; in other words, the use of shared storage limits the scalability of the VIM.

Finally, most of the schedulers are centralized, which also limits their scalability. In other words, they are unable to schedule a lot of virtual machines in a reasonably short time frame, especially if they have to take into account the resources of plenty of nodes.

3.5.2. *Interfaces*

This centralization problem also exists for VIMs graphical user interfaces, which are not designed to manage thousands of virtual machines and hundreds of nodes [KOT 10]. Administrators would then be wise to use command line tools.

Moreover, the Amazon EC2 API is partially supported (or even not supported at all) by the VIMs studied in this chapter. In particular, application automatic scaling is currently proposed only by Nimbus to FutureGrid users.

3.6. Conclusion

In this chapter, we studied the main VIMs that are deployed in production: Eucalyptus [NUR 09], Nimbus [NIM 13], OpenNebula [SOT 09], SCVMM [MIC 12], vCloud [VMW 10], vSphere [VMW 11], XenServer [CIT 12], CloudStack [APA 12] and OpenStack [OPE 12].

We first concentrated on how the VIMs organized distributed infrastructure resources. We observed that the VIMs were able to manage infrastructures ranging from a cluster to a data center or even a federation of data centers. This organization enabled infrastructure owners and users to benefit from increased flexibility.

We then focused on virtual machine scheduling. We noticed that most of the schedulers were centralized, that virtual machines were often scheduled in a static way, and that the most common scheduling policies were load balancing and consolidation.

We highlighted the advantages of using virtualization, for infrastructure owners and users. We mentioned in particular the possibility of isolating users from one another, of improving application scalability and of restarting virtual machines automatically in case of crashes, which was essential for applications that have to be highly available.

Finally, we noticed that the VIMs studied in this chapter had drawbacks, especially regarding interfaces and scheduling. We emphasized that they were centralized, which limited their ability to scale, in other words to manage large-scale infrastructures.

In the following chapters, we will focus on improving the scalability of VIMs, by studying the possibility to decentralize some management tasks.

Toward a Cooperative and Decentralized Framework to Manage Virtual Infrastructures

4

Comparative Study Between Virtual Infrastructure Managers and Distributed Operating Systems

In the previous chapters, we studied the management of distributed infrastructures before and after the rise of system virtualization. We mentioned that this rise had led to the development of new management frameworks. Moreover, we concluded that, even if these virtual infrastructure managers (VIMs) proposed advanced features to use resources more easily and efficiently, they were often highly centralized, which limited their ability to scale.

One solution to this problem is to decentralize the processing of management tasks. Similar issues have already been addressed by the research on distributed operating systems (DOS). Therefore, it would be interesting to determine whether the results of this research could help improving VIMs, in the same way as research on operating systems and hypervisors proved to be complementary at the level of a single node [HAN 05, HEI 06, ROS 07]. In this chapter, we propose to answer such a question by:

– developing the comparisons previously initiated between operating systems and hypervisors at the level of a single node [HAN 05, HEI 06, ROS 07];

– extending this study to a distributed context, to analyze whether some concepts implemented in DOSes can be applied to VIMs.

This study is a revised and extended version of one of our articles [QUE 11].

4.1. Comparison in the context of a single node

In this section, we focus on the management of local resources, by comparing the features provided by general purpose operating systems (GPOSs) and hypervisors, regarding the management of processes and virtual machines (VMs), their scheduling and the management of memory. To avoid repetitions when it is not necessary to draw the distinction, we will use the term *task* to refer to a process (respectively a VM), and the term *manager* to refer to a GPOS (respectively a hypervisor).

4.1.1. *Task lifecycle*

A manager has to manage tasks throughout their lifecycle, and to let them execute privilege instructions.

4.1.1.1. *Management of task lifecycle*

A manager can create new tasks by loading to memory appropriate instructions from a local or distant storage space.

Once a new task is created, the manager adds it to the list of tasks to be scheduled; the task is executed as soon as the scheduler selects it.

Before its completion, the scheduler can decide to pre-empt it to let another task run. This operation is called a *context switch*. It consists of saving the values stored in the processor registries by the running task, and to load the registry values associated with the task to run.

A task can also wait for a given event (for example, the termination of a read or write operation on the hard disk drive) before resuming its execution; the scheduler then puts the task in a waiting queue.

Once a task is terminated, the manager ensures that it can no longer be selected by the scheduler, and frees the memory pages it used, so that they can be assigned to another task.

The lifecycle of a task is summarized in Figure 4.1.

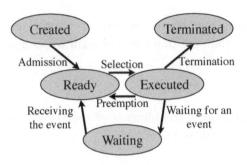

Figure 4.1. *Task lifecycle [SIL 98]*

4.1.1.2. *Execution of privileged instructions*

During its lifecycle, a task may need to execute privileged instructions; it then calls the manager.

A process uses a system call to the GPOS.

In the context of emulation or hardware virtualization, a guest GPOS executes instructions normally; however, in the case of paravirtualization, a guest GPOS uses a *hypercall*, in other words a system call to the hypervisor.

4.1.1.3. *Summary*

To sum up, GPOSes and hypervisors propose the same basic functionalities (creation, context switch, destruction and execution of privileged instructions), the former to manage processes and the latter to manage VMs.

4.1.2. *Scheduling*

Given that all tasks cannot be processed simultaneously by a single computing unit, the manager has to schedule them, to determine which task can be run at a given moment, how much processor it can use and for how long.

We will focus first on the schedulers of the most widely used GPOSes before studying those of the main hypervisors deployed in production.

4.1.2.1. *Windows*

Windows relies on a combination of round robin and priorities to schedule processes [WIN 13].

It always selects the process having the highest priority; if, while this process is running, another process gets a higher priority, the former is preempted to let the latter run.

All processes having the same priority are treated equally; each process is allowed to run for a fixed amount of time, before being preempted to let the next process run, like a round robin.

4.1.2.2. *Linux*

Linux default scheduler, the *completely fair scheduler* (CFS) [CFS 13] manages conventional time-shared processes by using an indicator – the virtual runtime – of the time a process has run. The virtual runtime is pondered by the number of runnable processes and by the process priority. CFS always executes the process that has the lowest virtual runtime, until it finds another process with a lower virtual runtime.

Each processor has its own set of processes to run; CFS tries to guarantee that the number of waiting processes is approximately the same for each processor, to balance the workload [SCH 13].

CFS takes into account the affinity of a process for a given processor. This favors the use of processor caches, thus improving performance.

4.1.2.3. *KVM*

KVM relies on the Linux scheduler, CFS, since KVM VMs are implemented as standard Linux processes [KIV 07].

4.1.2.4. *Xen*

The concept of virtual runtime is quite similar to the one used by the historical Xen *borrowed virtual time* (BVT) scheduler [CHI 07]. The BVT scheduler records the runtime of each VM – pondered by its weight – to calculate a virtual time. A VM can decrease its effective time (effective time = virtual time − diminution) temporarily to be scheduled in priority, as the BVT scheduler always selects the VM having the lowest effective time.

Nowadays, the default Xen scheduler is the *credit scheduler* (CS) [CHI 07]. It associates each VM with:

– a weight, to specify which proportion of processor time the VM can use;

– a *cap*, to specify the maximum amount of processor time the VM can use.

CS periodically allocates credits to VMs, proportionally to their weight and their cap. CS schedules VMs using a round-robin policy. When a VM has exhausted its credits or its cap, it lets another VM run. As a result, VM with a low weight tends to consume its credits quickly, letting VMs with higher weights run.

4.1.2.5. *ESX*

ESX takes account, for each VM, of the ratio of its effective processor runtime to its share, in other words the time during which the VM is allowed to use the processor [VMW 09]. The VM having the lowest ratio is executed first.

There are several ways for an ESX user to influence the share allocated to a VM, by associating it with:

– a share; a VM having a share, which is twice as much as the one of another machine can use twice as much processor;

– a reservation of processor capacity; the scheduler guarantees that a VM with a reservation can have access at least to the reserved capacity;

– a limit on processor utilization; a VM cannot use more processor time than the limit the user fixed.

ESX ensures to balance the workload between processors, by migrating VMs from one processor to another; it prioritizes the migration of VMs with low processor utilization, to avoid impacting those that store data in processor caches.

4.1.2.6. *Hyper-V*

Hyper-V implements concepts that are similar to those presented for ESX, namely: the specification of a share, a reservation or a limit to influence the processor utilization of a VM [HYP 13].

4.1.2.7. *Summary*

We found similarities between schedulers of processes and of VMs, especially regarding the following concepts: preemption, round robin, priority of a process and weight/share assigned to a VM, virtual runtime, processor affinity and load balancing between processors.

In fact, the scheduling needs are so close that a hosted hypervisor would be better of relying on its host GPOS, like KVM does with Linux.

4.1.3. *Memory management*

Memory is another resource that requires careful management.

4.1.3.1. *Allocation*

Once a task is created, the manager has to allocate memory to it. Like for scheduling, a GPOS and a native hypervisor have their own allocator, while a hosted hypervisor relies on the allocator of the host GPOS.

4.1.3.2. *Paging*

A process does not manipulate physical memory addresses directly; otherwise it could conflict with another process. Instead, it uses virtual memory addresses.

Virtual memory is commonly implemented through paging [TAN 01]. In this context, the GPOS is in charge of building

- for each process - a page table containing the translation of virtual addresses into physical addresses.

Implementing paging for a hypervisor is more complicated. Similarly to a process in a GPOS, an unmodified guest GPOS must not have access to physical addresses, as it could conflict with another guest GPOS. Thus, a guest GPOS only maintains translation tables from guest virtual addresses to guest physical addresses. The hypervisor either maintains translation tables:

– from guest virtual addresses to host physical addresses in the context of *shadow paging* [SMI 05], which is an emulation technique;

– or from guest physical addresses to host physical addresses, in the context of nested paging [ADV 08], which requires virtualization hardware extensions on the x86 architecture.

4.1.3.3. *Memory sharing*

Paging can be used to share physical pages among several programs to reduce the memory footprint.

For example, when forking a new process, the parent process may share its memory pages with its child. Shared pages are write-protected; when one process tries to change the content of a page, it gets a private copy it can modify. This is called *copy-on-write* [TAN 01].

Moreover, processes generally share libraries.

They can even share more if the GPOS provides a *content-based page sharing* functionality, like *Kernel Shared Memory* (KSM) [ARC 09] for Linux. KSM compares the pages of two processes; if some pages have identical contents, KSM merges them; as for the fork of a process, a process trying to write to a shared page gets a mutable copy. It is worth noting that content-based page sharing was first implemented by hypervisors (see Chapter 2).

The interest of sharing memory increases greatly in the context of system virtualization. Several VMs may be present on the same node at the same time, each running a potentially identical guest GPOS, thus consuming a great amount of memory. This is, therefore, attractive if the hypervisor can merge identical pages owned by different VMs [WAL 02]. This functionality is implemented inside the hypervisor for a type I, and in the host GPOS for a type II.

4.1.3.4. *Swap*

When there is not enough memory, even if content-based page sharing is used, some pages need to be swapped out [TAN 01].

A GPOS tries to swap the least frequently used pages out, to avoid degrading performance too much.

Unfortunately, a hypervisor does not know which pages are used occasionally, contrary to its guest GPOSes. It can swap pages out randomly, but this is not efficient. The ballooning technique [WAL 02] was, therefore, created to solve this problem. It enables the hypervisor to communicate with the guest GPOSes to know the least frequently used pages (see Chapter 2).

4.1.3.5. *Summary*

To sum up, GPOSes and hypervisors tend nowadays to propose equivalent memory management functionalities, namely paging, memory allocation, memory sharing (especially content-based page sharing) and efficient swapping.

4.1.4. *Summary*

To conclude this section, we showed that hypervisors were really close to GPOSes in terms of mechanisms proposed at the level of a single node.

We observed that many features that had been first implemented by GPOSes were then provided by hypervisors. The reverse was also true, since content-based page sharing was first proposed by hypervisors before being implemented by a GPOS.

4.2. Comparison in a distributed context

In this section, we will extend the previous study on resource and task management to a distributed context.

We will, therefore, compare the features provided by DOS and VIMs.

4.2.1. *Task lifecycle*

Managing tasks implies being able to deploy them on the infrastructure, to migrate them from one node to another, and to take snapshots.

4.2.1.1. *Deployment of tasks*

DOSes can deploy processes in at least two ways, (1) by remote duplication of processes [GOS 02] or (2) by remote creation of processes [LIG 03]. Duplicating a process implies that the state of the parent process is transferred on the node where the child should be created. On the contrary, creating a process remotely means that a process is created on the destination node without cloning an existing process.

These facilities are similar to those implemented in some VIMs. The Snowflock project [CAV 09] thus proposes the distributed fork of VMs: A VM can be cloned into multiple replicas running on different physical machines; only some information is copied initially; a clone then retrieves memory pages on the first access, from an immutable memory image of the original VM. However, VIMs generally create VMs remotely; they must provide the destination node with the disk image of the VM, before actually creating it.

4.2.1.2. *Migration of tasks*

Once a task is deployed on a node, the manager may decide to migrate it to another node if necessary.

4.2.1.2.1. Migration of processes

Process migration [MIL 00] can be used to implement dynamic load balancing, to perform maintenance operations, or to make data access more efficient (by moving a process closer to its data which is located on another node).

There are two prerequisites to migrate a process. First, a process must have a unique identifier, to be identifiable wherever it is located in the cluster. Secondly, it is necessary to extract all pieces of information related to the process: registry values, address space and file descriptors. Once information is extracted, several techniques can be used to migrate the content of memory pages.

After migration, a process runs normally on the destination node. However, some system calls cannot be performed from this new location, as resources are not always available locally (there are *residual dependencies*). The main system calls concerned by this problem are related to the address space, interprocess communications, file and network accesses. Three possibilities exist to solve this issue:

– send a request to the node that is able to perform the system call;

– send a request to a distributed system that will deal with the system call;

– ask for a copy of the system resource to access it locally.

To sum up, process migration is an important feature proposed by DOSes, but it is hard to implement.

4.2.1.2.2. Migration of virtual machines

VM (live) migration [CLA 05] is easier to implement than process migration, since there are no residual dependencies on the source node. As a result, most hypervisors provide VM live migration.

Recent work has aimed at reducing the downtime inherent to migration by means of algorithms derived from those used for process migration [HIR 11].

4.2.1.3. *Snapshotting*

Taking a snapshot [CHA 85] is very similar to performing a migration, as it requires extracting information related to the process (respectively the VM). However, data are stored on the disk or in the memory, and not sent over the network. VM snapshotting is easier to implement than process snapshotting for the same reason as VM migration is easier to implement than process migration.

4.2.1.4. *Summary*

To summarize, VIMs have drawn their inspiration from DOSes to propose mechanisms related to the management of VMs, such as deployment, migration and snapshotting. It is worth noting that migration and snapshotting mechanisms are easier to implement for VMs than for processes.

As strong similarities already exist between DOSes and VIMs, the literature on DOSes does not seem to help to improve the management of virtual machines in a distributed context.

4.2.2. Scheduling

Deployment, migration and snapshotting mechanisms may be used by the global scheduler, especially if it performs task dynamic scheduling.

4.2.2.1. *Dynamic scheduling and distributed operating systems*

DOSes (such as OpenMosix, OpenSSI and Kerrighed [LOT 05]) mainly rely on dynamic scheduling to perform load balancing, by migrating processes from overloaded nodes to less loaded ones.

The migration may be initiated either by a sender node, a receiver node or by both of them [TAN 01].

In the sender-initiated policy, an overloaded node (the sender) tries, by probing nodes randomly, to find a less loaded node to give it some processes.

The situation is exactly the opposite in the receiver-initiated policy, where an underloaded node (the receiver) probes nodes randomly to find an overloaded one.

Finally, in the symmetric policy, a node can ask for more processes or try to get rid of them, depending on its load.

4.2.2.2. *Dynamic scheduling and virtual infrastructure managers*

Contrary to DOSes, most of the VIMs implementing dynamic scheduling (such as Entropy [HER 09, HER 11], vSphere [VMW 11] and SCVMM [MIC 12]) follow a centralized approach, where a single node is in charge of scheduling virtual machines for the whole infrastructure.

Recently, several proposals suggested more decentralized approaches [YAZ 10, MAS 11, ROU 11, FEL 12c]. However, the corresponding prototypes still relied on centralized points (e.g. for data collection of infrastructure resources). We will detail these approaches in the next chapter.

Currently, as shown in Chapter 3, load balancing and consolidation are the most common scheduling policies implemented by VIMs.

4.2.2.3. *Summary*

To summarize, VIMs could be improved regarding dynamic task scheduling in a distributed context with the results of research on DOSes. Indeed, the former generally follow a centralized approach, whereas the latter have dropped it years ago in favor of a decentralized one.

4.2.3. *Memory management*

We saw how scheduling mechanisms could be extended to a distributed context; now, we focus on the memory management.

Two solutions were presented in the literature regarding the global management of memory: global scheduling and distributed shared memory.

4.2.3.1. *Through scheduling*

We saw in section 4.1.3 that content-based page sharing could help reducing the amount of memory used on a node; this functionality has in fact an equivalent for VMs in a distributed context, which was implemented by the Memory Buddies project [WOO 09].

The main idea is that each guest GPOS analyses the memory content of the VM it is running on, and sends the information to a front-end.

The front-end then observes which VMs could share memory if they were running on the same node, and performs appropriate migrations to group VMs by memory affinities.

Finally, hypervisors use content-based page sharing to effectively reduce the amount of memory used within each node, by merging identical memory pages.

To the best of our knowledge, DOSes do not have a functionality similar to the one proposed by the Memory Buddies project.

4.2.3.2. *Through distributed shared memory*

Distributed shared memory is another key feature for the global management of memory in distributed systems, as it provides "the shared memory abstraction on physically distributed memory machines" [ESK 96].

This very popular research topic has been applied to DOSes, and more specifically to those aiming at creating single system images (such as OpenMosix, OpenSSI and Kerrighed). However, this abstraction is not widely used by VIMs. It was implemented in vNUMA [CHA 09] and ScaleMP vSMP Foundation [VSM 13], two hypervisors that aggregate processor and memory resources of several homogeneous nodes. It is worth noting that this approach was validated on a small-scale infrastructure; vNUMA was evaluated with eight nodes, whereas ScaleMP certifies that its hypervisor can aggregate the resources of up to 128 nodes.

4.2.3.3. *Summary*

To sum up, research on VIMs seems to be ahead of research on DOSes in terms of global memory management, since it addressed not only distributed shared memory but also distributed content-based page sharing.

However, most VIMs do not implement distributed content-based page sharing. Moreover, the existing prototype is based on a centralized approach, which limits its ability to scale.

4.2.4. *Summary*

In summary, VIMs propose several functionalities that are similar to those existing in DOSes for the management of tasks and resources in a distributed context.

However, the former could be improved (1) by generalizing the implementation of global memory management mechanisms and (2) by decentralizing scheduling.

4.3. Conclusion

In this chapter, we have compared the management features provided by VIMs and DOS, at the level of a single node and in a distributed context. We focused on the management of tasks' lifecycle and on their scheduling.

We first developed the reflections initiated by previous work regarding operating systems and hypervisors [HAN 05, HEI 06, ROS 07]. We established the fact that (1) there are similarities between these two kinds of managers and that (2) one research field could benefit from progress made in the other.

We then extended our study to a distributed context, which resulted in identifying potential contributions, especially regarding the decentralization of VM dynamic scheduling.

We will study this point in more detail in the following chapters. We will first describe existing approaches extensively, before presenting our own approach.

5

Dynamic Scheduling of
Virtual Machines

The comparison between virtual infrastructure managers and distributed operating systems enabled us to identify some potential contributions regarding the former, especially on the decentralization of the dynamic scheduling of VMs.

In this chapter, we will recall some design choices that have an impact on scheduler architectures. We will then detail the limits of a centralized approach. Finally, we will study the approaches proposed in the literature to decentralize the scheduling of VMs, distinguishing between hierarchical and multiagent approaches.

5.1. Scheduler architectures

The dynamic scheduling of VMs is interesting when taking account of the fluctuations of workload, to optimize their placement. There are three main steps in dynamic scheduling. The first step is related to monitoring: the scheduler retrieves data on worker node resources and on their use by VMs. The second step is the decision one: the scheduler computes a reconfiguration plan from the data collected, in other words a list of operations (for example migrations) to be performed on VMs. Finally, the reconfiguration plan is applied in the third step.

There are several possibilities to perform these different steps. We will focus on monitoring and decision-making. In fact, applying a reconfiguration plan simply consists of sending migration orders to the hypervisors.

5.1.1. *Monitoring*

Several choices have to be made regarding the monitoring of the infrastructure [ROT 94].

First, it is mandatory to specify which nodes are in charge of collecting the information: a single dedicated service node, in the context of a centralized architecture, several service nodes organized in a hierarchical way or all worker nodes, in the context of a multiagent approach.

It is then necessary to determine which worker nodes are involved during each collection operation: all, some of them or a variable number.

It is also required to specify whether the worker nodes are volunteers in the collection process, in other words if they choose when to send information to the collector, or if they only answer to the requests of the latter.

If the worker nodes are volunteers, it is necessary to specify when they send information to the collector: periodically or only when some conditions regarding the state of their resources are met.

5.1.2. *Decision-making*

The decision-making step also requires making some choices [ROT 94].

It is especially required to determine which nodes are in charge of making decisions. Once again, it is possible to rely on a centralized, hierarchical or multiagent approach.

In the context of a multiagent approach, it is then necessary to specify which nodes make decisions, to avoid conflicting actions. This may require implementing a synchronization mechanism.

5.2. Limits of a centralized approach

As shown in Chapters 3 and 4, virtual infrastructure managers that are able to dynamically schedule VMs are more likely to rely on a centralized and periodic approach (see Figure 5.1).

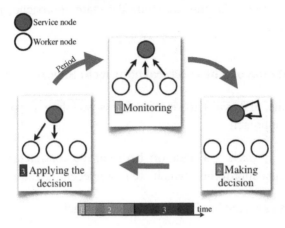

Figure 5.1. *Centralized periodic dynamic scheduling*

Each scheduling step takes some time, those related to computing and applying a reconfiguration plan being the longest ones. The more nodes and VMs a scheduler has to manage, the longer the duration of these steps will be. Nowadays, infrastructures tend to be bigger and bigger; for instance, two main actors of cloud computing, Rackspace and OVH, announced that they had, respectively, 80,000 and 120,000 nodes [WHO 13].

Centralized schedulers in charge of large-scale infrastructures cannot react quickly when some nodes are overloaded, which may lead to a degradation of the quality of service expected by users.

Moreover, the longer the reconfiguration step is, the more the VMs' workloads are likely to change; therefore, the reconfiguration plan is outdated before being fully applied.

Finally, the node hosting the scheduler is a single point of failure: if it crashes, or if the network connection with the other nodes is cut, there is no scheduling anymore.

One way to mitigate these problems consists of decentralizing scheduling. In the following, we study the main approaches presented in the literature.

5.3. Presentation of a hierarchical approach: Snooze

One of the first ways to decentralize scheduling is to rely on a hierarchical approach.

Such an approach is a trade-off between the centralized approach and multiagents approaches, which are more decentralized.

Snooze is an example of a hierarchical approach.

5.3.1. *Presentation*

The Snooze [FEL 12a, FEL 12c] hierarchical approach relies on three layers that are made of:
- local controllers (LC);
- group managers (GM);
- group leader (GL).

Each node hosts an LC. When they start, LCs are distributed across several GMs (each GM runs on its own service node); an LC searches for another GM only if its GM crashes; each LC periodically sends information to its GM regarding the state of its resources and the VMs it hosts. GMs are supervised by a GL (the GL being elected among the GMs; it delegates the management of its LCs to other GMs); each GM periodically sends aggregated information to the GL on the LCs it is in charge of (see Figure 5.2).

Snooze takes account of processor, memory and network resources during scheduling.

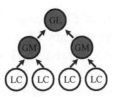

Figure 5.2. *Snooze – monitoring*

Several factors can trigger scheduling:

– the creation of a new VM; the GL chooses which GM will place the VM, and the GM then chooses on which node to start the VM;

– the periodic optimization of a criterion specified by the administrator (for instance, to perform consolidation); each GM periodically tries to optimize this criterion among the nodes it is in charge of;

– node overloads or underloads; the corresponding LC notifies its GM, and the latter tries to solve the problem.

The prototype was evaluated under real conditions on the Grid'5000 test bed, through an experiment that involved 500 VMs distributed across 136 worker nodes.

5.3.2. *Discussion*

Snooze is able to distribute the scheduling work between several GMs, while ensuring that scheduling can continue in case one of the system components fails.

However, its architecture is still partially centralized, since the GL has a global (yet simplified) view of the infrastructure, and because it has to manage every VM creation request, which can limit its scalability.

Moreover, the evaluation focused on VM creation requests, without studying periodic optimizations or even the processing of overloaded and underloaded node problems.

Finally, the distribution of LCs across GMs may lead to several issues. If a GM is in charge of many LCs, the scheduling process can take a long time and may not be reactive. However, if a GM supervises few LCs, there are fewer opportunities to migrate VMs, and the GM may not be able to solve overloaded node problems. One improvement (that was proposed but not implemented, to the best of our knowledge) would consist of letting GMs cooperate with one another if case one GM cannot find a solution.

5.4. Presentation of multiagent approaches

Other proposals were elaborated to further decentralize the scheduling work. These approaches are said to be multiagent approaches, since they rely on the installation of a software agent on each node of the infrastructure, the scheduling work being distributed across the agents.

5.4.1. *A bio-inspired algorithm for energy optimization in a self-organizing data center [BAR 10]*

5.4.1.1. *Presentation*

This approach aims at optimizing the energy consumption of the infrastructure. The scheduling algorithm is similar to a consolidation algorithm.

In this approach, each agent can send one or several scouts. A scout is a software entity that travels on the neighbor nodes to collect information on available resources. Once a scout is back to its origin node, it shares its information with the local agent. The agent then decides whether it is relevant to offload some of the VMs hosted locally on to another node; this is more likely to happen if the node is slightly loaded (and *vice versa*). In the case of a migration, the agent chooses the destination node that consumes the least energy and the resources (processor and memory) that are used the most. The origin node is shut down if it does not host any VM.

This approach was validated through simulations involving more than 1,000 worker nodes. The number of VMs was not specified in the corresponding article.

5.4.1.2. *Discussion*

This approach is original, since (to the best of our knowledge) it is the first approach to completely decentralize the scheduling of VMs: each agent has a partial view of the infrastructure and is only in charge of the VMs hosted on its node. Moreover, this approach is fault-tolerant: if a scout disappears following a node crash, its origin node only has to send another scout to let scheduling continue.

However, its designers observed that this approach led to many migrations. They also highlighted that it is necessary to limit the number of nodes a scout can keep information on, in order to use less network bandwidth. Moreover, the experimental results showed that the consolidation rate was quite far from the optimal rate. Furthermore, information collected by the scouts could be outdated when they come back to their origin node: some VMs could have migrated during their travel, and VM consumptions of resources could have fluctuated. In addition, it seems that no synchronization mechanism was implemented to prevent several nodes from sending, simultaneously, their VMs to the same destination node, which could lead to overload problems. Finally, this approach does not take account of sequential dependencies: the migration of a VM may first require moving another VM before being performed.

5.4.2. *Dynamic resource allocation in computing clouds through distributed multiple criteria decision analysis [YAZ 10]*

5.4.2.1. *Presentation*

This approach implements a consolidation algorithm.

In this approach, a scheduling process is triggered only when an agent detects that the resources of its nodes are overloaded or underloaded. In the first case, it tries to get rid of a VM to stay below the overload threshold; in the second case, it tries to migrate all VMs from its node to other nodes. For each VM to be migrated, the agent contacts a mediator (which is in charge of collecting information on the state of node resources); the mediator sends, to the agent, a list of nodes with enough available resources to host the VM to be migrated; the agent then chooses the node with the least available resources (processor, memory and network).

This approach was validated through simulations that involved up to 20,000 VMs and 2,500 worker nodes.

5.4.2.2. *Discussion*

This approach implements a synchronization mechanism to prevent several nodes from sending, simultaneously, their VMs to the same destination node. Moreover, the simulations showed that this approach could dramatically decrease the number of VM migrations, compared to a centralized heuristic approach; however, this objective was reached by sacrificing the consolidation rate.

Moreover, even if this approach is indeed decentralized regarding decision-making, data collection is performed in a centralized way, which limits scalability and fault-tolerance (if the mediator crashes, the agents cannot migrate VMs anymore).

Finally, this approach does not manage sequential dependencies for VM migrations.

5.4.3. *Server consolidation in clouds through gossiping [MAR 11]*

5.4.3.1. *Presentation*

This approach implements a consolidation algorithm.

Each agent communicates periodically with its neighbors (the neighborhood is changed periodically and randomly). On each communication, the node with the least VMs sends as many VMs as possible to the other node.

This approach was evaluated trough simulations that involved 40,000 VMs and 10,000 worker nodes.

5.4.3.2. *Discussion*

This approach is fully decentralized. Moreover, it is fault-tolerant: if a node crashes, the other nodes can still exchange VMs. In addition, this approach is able to come close to the optimal consolidation rate.

However, it does not take account of the heterogeneity of VMs, and, more importantly, it does not take account of their consumption of resources, which has an impact on the migration cost. Moreover, this approach cannot handle overloaded node problems. Furthermore, it leads to many migrations [FEL 12b]. Finally, this approach does not manage sequential dependencies for VM migrations.

5.4.4. *Self-economy in cloud data centers – statistical assignment and migration of virtual machines [MAS 11]*

5.4.4.1. *Presentation*

This approach implements a consolidation algorithm.

A service node handles VM creation requests. For this purpose, the node communicates with all agents to decide where to place a new VM. Each agent then uses a probability function to determine whether it is relevant for its node to host the new VM; if so, the agent notifies the service node. The service node then randomly chooses one of the worker nodes that notified it, in order to place the VM.

Moreover, each agent regularly uses another probability function to decide if it would be interesting to migrate one or more VMs from its node to other nodes. The probability to migrate a VM increases when the processor utilization rate of a node (1) exceeds an overload threshold, or (2) goes below an underload threshold. The agent then chooses a VM to migrate and contact the service node to decide where to place it, as in the case of a new VM creation request.

This approach was evaluated by means of simulations that involved up to 2,400 VMs and 100 worker nodes.

5.4.4.2. *Discussion*

This approach is decentralized regarding the collection of information on worker nodes; however, the choice of the destination node for a VM is made in a centralized way. This approach prevents some nodes from sending their VMs simultaneously to the same destination node. However, it can also lead to problems related to fault-tolerance (if the service node crashes) or scalability (the service node has to handle many requests when the utilization rate of the infrastructure is close to the maximum, since the number of migrations increases exponentially, as shown by the experimental results). Finally, this approach does not manage sequential dependencies for VM migrations.

5.4.5. *A distributed and collaborative dynamic load balancer for virtual machines [ROU 11]*

5.4.5.1. *Presentation*

This approach was designed for load balancing.

A scheduling operation is triggered when (1) a new VM is created; (2) the resources (CPU and memory) of a node are overused, or (3) a node is put into maintenance mode. The scheduling task is then added to a waiting queue on the node where it has been created. This scheduling task can be processed either by the local agent, or by an agent on another node, by means of a work stealing mechanism; we will assume that the scheduling task is processed locally, to simplify the explanations. In the case of an event linked with the overutilization of the resources of a node, the agent does not know at first which VM to migrate; it starts to gather information on local VMs, before selecting the virtual machine that consumes the least amount of resources to migrate it. Once the agent knows which VM to migrate, it has to find a destination; thus, it collects information on all nodes of the infrastructure, before selecting the node that has the most available resources. The agent finally migrates the selected VM on the destination node.

This approach was evaluated by means of simulations that involved up to 1,000 VMs and 140 nodes.

5.4.5.2. *Discussion*

This approach presents the following advantages: (1) it balances the load well between nodes and (2) it is fault-tolerant; if a node is faulty, it would not prevent other nodes from scheduling the remaining VMs.

However, for each scheduling task, the steps related to information gathering and decision-making requires us to take account of all nodes of the infrastructure, which limits the scalability of this approach.

Moreover, the decision may not be appropriate, since the state of the resources on the destination node may have changed; this implies starting a new scheduling process to find a solution.

Finally, this approach does not manage sequential dependencies for VM migrations.

5.4.6. *A case for fully decentralized dynamic virtual machine consolidation in clouds [FEL 12b]*

5.4.6.1. *Presentation*

This approach improves the proposal presented in [MAR 11] to perform consolidation.

Like before, each node only knows the nodes inside its neighborhood; this neighborhood changes periodically and randomly. However, nodes do not communicate two by two to exchange VMs. Instead, each agent periodically tries to reserve all nodes inside its neighborhood; it fails if one of them has already been reserved by another agent; however, if it succeeds, it then becomes responsible of scheduling the VMs inside its neighborhood. For this purpose, it gathers information on resources (CPU, memory and network) consumed by the VMs; the way VMs are relocated depends on the consolidation algorithm. Once scheduling is over, the agent frees the nodes so that another agent can reserve them.

This approach was evaluated using several consolidation algorithms, including the one presented in [MAR 11]. This evaluation was carried out by means of simulations that involved up to 6,048 VMs and 1,008 nodes.

5.4.6.2. *Discussion*

Like [MAR 11], this approach is decentralized and partially fault-tolerant. As a matter of fact, the crash of a node does not halt scheduling; however, the crash of the node in charge of scheduling the VMs inside a neighborhood does put an end to the scheduling inside this neighborhood; moreover, since the nodes were reserved for scheduling and will not be freed, they cannot be reserved by subsequent scheduling processes once they are distributed among other neighborhoods; thus, every attempt to schedule VMs inside these neighborhoods will fail. This problem reveals another weakness of this approach: it requires a more sophisticated algorithm to elect a leader inside each neighborhood to guarantee fast and deadlock-free leader elections.

Contrary to [MAR 11], this approach takes account of the real resource consumption of VMs and enables us to overbook resources. However, this approach does not handle overload situations efficiently, since scheduling is performed periodically inside neighborhoods of fixed size: the scheduling period equals to 30 s, and if it is not possible to solve the problem inside the current neighborhood, we have to wait until the neighborhood has changed before trying again to find a solution.

Finally, once again, this approach does not manage sequential dependencies for VM migrations.

5.5. Conclusion

In this chapter, we studied several approaches to schedule VMs dynamically (see Tables 5.1 and 5.2). We focused on fault-tolerance and scalability, in other words, the ability to efficiently manage infrastructures composed of many nodes and VMs.

We first recalled some design choices that have an impact on scheduler architectures, especially regarding monitoring and decision-making.

We then presented the limits of a centralized approach, which cannot quickly solve quality of service violations, so that a reconfiguration plan can be outdated before being fully applied.

Afterward, we detailed Snooze [FEL 12a, FEL 12c], an example of hierarchical architecture that distributes the scheduling work over several software entities, which is fault-tolerant but still partially centralized.

We finally addressed multiagent approaches, which distribute the scheduling work over all nodes composing the infrastructure [BAR 10, YAZ 10, MAR 11, MAS 11, ROU 11, FEL 12b]. Nevertheless, we highlighted several limitations. Regarding scalability, some approaches require a global knowledge of the infrastructure to make a decision [YAZ 10, ROU 11], and/or resort to a centralized service node [YAZ 10, MAS 11]. This service node is not fault-tolerant and its crash puts an end to VM scheduling on the infrastructure. Scheduling sometimes leads to many VM migrations [BAR 10, MAR 11], without necessarily optimizing the chosen scheduling criterion [BAR 10]. Furthermore, these approaches do not manage sequential dependencies for VM migrations. Finally, [FEL 12b] cannot quickly solve overload problems in the context of an overbooked infrastructure.

In our opinion, an ideal decentralized approach to schedule VMs dynamically should:
- be able to manage overbooked infrastructures;
- be extremely reactive to solve overload problems;
- find solutions with quality equivalent to that obtained with a centralized approach;
- limit the number of VM migrations to perform;
- manage sequential dependencies when applying a reconfiguration plan;

– implement an efficient synchronization mechanism to avoid conflicts when simultaneously applying several reconfiguration plans;

– work well when nodes are added to or removed from the infrastructure.

We designed the Distributed VM Scheduler (DVMS) proposal with these objectives in mind. We present DVMS in the next chapter.

Name	Scheduling Triggers	Scheduling Policies	Resources Considered for Scheduling
[BAR 10]	Return of a scout on it origin node	Energy optimization (≈ consolidation)	*CPU *Memory *Energy consumption
[YAZ 10]	*VM creation *Node overload *Node underload	Consolidation	*CPU *Memory *Network bandwidth
[MAR 11]	Period	Consolidation	Number of hosted VMs
[MAS 11]	*VM creation *Node overload *Node underload	Consolidation	CPU
[ROU 11]	*VM creation *Node overload *Maintenance operation on a node	Load balancing	*CPU *Memory
Snooze	*VM creation *Node overload *Node underload *Period	*VM creation: round-robin *Overload, underload, period: not evaluated	*CPU *Memory *Network
[FEL 12b]	Period (30 seconds)	Consolidation	*CPU *Memory *Network

Table 5.1. *Academic approaches to schedule VMs dynamically (1/2)*

Name	Selection of a Virtual Machine (VM) to Migrate	Selection of a Destination Node	Characteristics of the Biggest Experiment
[BAR 10]	1) Information gathering on VMs hosted locally 2) Selection of VMs that can and should migrate on one of the nodes visited by a scout	1) Information gathering on nodes collected by the scouts 2) Selection of the node with the lowest energy consumption and with the highest load	*Simulation *1,000 nodes
[YAZ 10]	1) Information gathering on VMs hosted locally 2a) Overload situation: Selection of the VM that enables to stay below the overload threshold 2b) Underload situation: All VMs hosted locally	1) Information gathering, by means of the mediator, on all nodes that can host the VM 2) Selection of the node with the least amount of available resources	*Simulation *20,000 VMs / 2,500 nodes
[MAR 11]	1) Communication with one of the 20 nodes composing the neighborhood (rebuilt randomly every x seconds) 2) The node with the fewest VMs sends extra VMs to the other node	See selection of a VM to migrate	*Simulation *40,000 VMs / 10,000 nodes
[MAS 11]	1) Information gathering on VMs hosted locally 2) Selection of the VM?	1) The mediator asks each node if it can hosts the VM 2) Only the nodes that can host the VM answer 3) The mediator randomly chooses a node among them	*Simulation *2,400 VMs / 100 nodes
[ROU 11]	1) Information gathering on VMs hosted locally 2) Selection of the VMs with the lowest needs for resources	1) Information gathering on all nodes 2) Selection of the node with the highest amount of available resources	*Simulation *1,000 VMs / 140 nodes
Snooze	1) Local controllers periodically (every 10s) send information on their VMs to their group leader 2) The group leader infers which VMs to migrate	1) Local controllers periodically (every 10s) send information on their node to their group leader 2) The group leader infers on which nodes the VMs should be migrated	*Experiment on a real test bed *500 VMs / 136 nodes
[FEL 12b]	1) Information gathering on the VMs hosted on the 16 nodes composing the neighborhood (randomly rebuilt every 10s) 2) The selection of the VM depends on the algorithm used; ACO tends to favor VMs with the highest needs for resources	1) Information gathering on the 16 nodes composing the neighborhood 2) The selection of the node depends on the algorithm used; ACO tends to favor nodes with the lowest needs for resources	*Simulation *6,048 VMs / 1,008 nodes

Table 5.2. *Academic approaches to schedule VMs dynamically (2/2)*

DVMS, a Cooperative and Decentralized Framework to Dynamically Schedule Virtual Machines

6

DVMS: A Proposal to Schedule Virtual Machines in a Cooperative and Reactive Way

In the previous chapter, we studied the contributions related to autonomous, dynamic and decentralized virtual machine (VM) scheduling.

Even though significant progress has been achieved, we showed that there was no approach able at the same time to (1) manage overbooked infrastructures, (2) solve the overload problems quickly, (3) find quality solutions, which are comparable to those obtained with a centralized approach, (4) limit the number of migrations, (5) manage sequential dependencies, (6) prevent conflicts due to the application of several reconfiguration plans simultaneously, (7) take account of node additions or removals.

Keeping these principles in mind, we designed a new approach, distributed virtual machine scheduler (DVMS). The DVMS is deployed as a network of agents organized following a ring topology, and that cooperates with one another to quickly process events (related to overloaded or underloaded nodes) that occur on the infrastructure. DVMS can process several events simultaneously and independently by dynamically partitioning the infrastructure, each partition having an appropriate size regarding the event it is associated with.

In this chapter, we detail the fundamental ideas behind DVMS and we present their implementation in a prototype. This chapter is a revised and extended version of two of our articles [QUE 12, QUE 13].

6.1. DVMS fundamentals

6.1.1. *Working hypotheses*

We worked with the following hypotheses regarding the infrastructure to manage:

1) Nodes can be identical or different.

2) Each node can communicate with any other node, through the network.

3) Each node hosts a hypervisor; this hypervisor is the same for all nodes.

4) VMs are heterogeneous; we manipulate them as black boxes; we only know their CPU and memory consumption.

5) Each VM can be migrated on any node; this implies that:

- each node can get access to each VM disk image, either through a shared storage area or by migrating all or part of the disk image when it is necessary;

- the network bandwidth is sufficient to quickly migrate a VM (within seconds);

- even if the nodes do not have the same model of central processing unit (CPU), the hypervisor can still perform migrations, like the kernel-based virtual machine (KVM) does.

From a software point of view, the nodes are organized following a ring topology. This topology guarantees that, if a message emitted by a node needs to traverse all nodes of the infrastructure, it would traverse each node only once before going back to its sender.

Concretely, this message is an event; a scheduling procedure is started as soon as an event occurs on the infrastructure, so that it can quickly process the event. We will focus on events related to overloaded or underloaded nodes. The system administrator can define these events by means of thresholds.

Each event is associated with a partition.

DEFINITION 6.1.– Partition – *A partition is composed of all the nodes that are reserved for the resolution of a specific event.*

Partitioning the infrastructure is mandatory to avoid conflicts between several schedulers when they apply their reconfiguration plans. Suppose that two schedulers S_1 and S_2 could manipulate the same VMs and that S_1 found a reconfiguration plan before S_2; the reconfiguration plan found by S_1 could invalidate the plan found by S_2 if S_1 either (1) migrated some VMs that S_2 would have moved too, or if S_1 (2) used resources that would have been necessary so that S_2 could perform some migrations; therefore, S_2 would have spent time computing a reconfiguration plan with no concrete result, since this plan would be unusable; we want to avoid this situation.

Each partition includes two special nodes, the initiator and the leader.

DEFINITION 6.2.– Initiator – *The initiator of a partition is the node that initially produced the event associated with this partition.*

DEFINITION 6.3.– Leader – *The leader of a partition is the node that leads the scheduling computations aiming at solving the event associated with this partition; the leader of the partition is likely to change during the processing of the event.*

6.1.2. *Presentation of the event processing procedure*

The event processing procedure [QUE 12] is initiated when a node N_i observes that there is a problem, for instance when its resources are overused (see Figures 6.1, 6.2); it then generates an event and reserves itself to process this event (see Figure 6.2(a)). After that it forwards this event to its neighbor on the ring, node N_{i+1}.

If N_{i+1} is already involved in another partition, it directly forwards the event to node N_{i+2}; otherwise, N_{i+1} joins the new partition (see Figure 6.2(b)) and checks that the event is still valid. If the event is not valid anymore (for instance because the VMs's demands for resources fluctuated), N_{i+1} cancels the reservations to destroy the partition and thus allow the nodes that composed it to take part to other event processing procedures. On the contrary, if the event is still valid, N_{i+1} notifies all the nodes inside the partition that it is the new leader; in return, it receives information regarding (1) the capacities of each node and (2) the resources consumed by the VMs hosted on each node. It then starts a scheduling computation; if no solution is found, the event is then forwarded to node N_{i+2}.

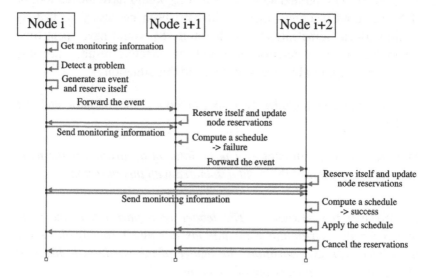

Figure 6.1. *Event processing procedure*

N_{i+2} repeats the same operations, that is to say: self-reservation (if it is free, see Figure 6.2(c)), event validity check, leader change notification, monitoring of VMs and nodes inside the partition, scheduling computation. If N_{i+2} finds a solution, it applies the corresponding reconfiguration plan that solves the event; it then cancels reservations to destroy the partition and thus allow the nodes that composed it to take part to other event processing procedures.

Note that if N_{i+2} did not find a solution, the partition would have grown until a solution is found or the event had traversed the whole ring. In the latter case, the problem would be considered as unsolvable and the partition would be destroyed; this behavior is not ideal, and we will propose a way to improve it.

The increase progressing in size of the partition aims at adapting it to the complexity of the problem to solve. This approach enables us to consider the smallest number of nodes as possible, thus accelerating the scheduling computations to solve the event as quickly as possible.

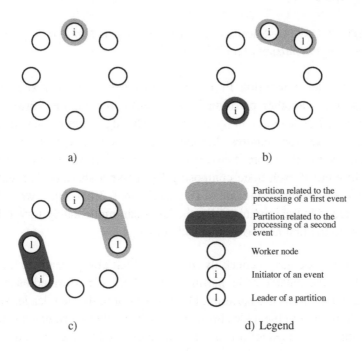

Figure 6.2. *Processing two events simultaneously*

Note that a scheduling computation can take account of more than two nodes at the same time, to provide a scheduler that manages sequential dependencies with more possibilities to migrate VMs.

Note also that on each leader change, the new leader gathers information on the resources of each node; this is necessary because VMs' needs for resources can fluctuate during the lifetime of a partition.

Finally, observe that several events can be processed simultaneously and independently, as shown in Figures 6.2(b) and 6.2(c).

6.1.3. *Acceleration of the ring traversal*

We studied several ways to improve event processing; the first one consisted of defining *shortcuts* to accelerate the traversal of the ring [QUE 13].

DEFINITION 6.4.– Shortcut – *A shortcut is a direct path to the first node that is on the outside of a partition.*

Consider a partition P_1 (in gray) that needs to grow and that is adjacent to another partition P_2 (in black), see Figure 6.3(a); P_2 is composed of several contiguous nodes. The algorithm presented in the previous section requires that event E_1 associated with P_1 traverses each node in P_2 before it arrives on a free node. However, the situation is different if each node composing P_2 knows a shortcut that leads to the first node on the outside of P_2 (see Figure 6.3(b)). Thus, when E_1 is forwarded to the initiator of P_2, the latter can immediately forward this event to the first node on the outside of P_2.

Each node has to check its shortcut, which always leads to the first node on the outside of its partition; this check is performed each time a new node joins the partition. On this occasion, the new leader shares its shortcut with the nodes inside the partition; this shortcut leads to the neighbor of the leader (or to the node referenced by the shortcut of the neighbor, if the latter is involved in the same partition as the leader); a node updates its shortcut only if it led to the node that became the new leader. This selective update enables us to handle situations where the partition is not composed of contiguous nodes (see Figure 6.3(c)); for instance, the first two nodes inside partition P_1 keep their shortcut leading to the initiator of partition P_2, while the shortcut of the leader of P_1 leads to the last free node.

6.1.4. *Guarantee that a solution will be found if it exists*

Another improvement to the event processing procedure is to guarantee that a solution will always be found if it exists [QUE 13].

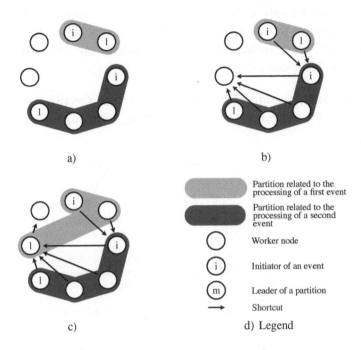

Figure 6.3. *Using shortcuts to accelerate the traversal of the ring*

6.1.4.1. *Prerequisites*

The first step consists of avoiding the destruction of a partition when the corresponding event comes back to the initiator without being solved; it is indeed plausible that some nodes, which were previously involved in other partitions, are now free and could be used to solve this event.

However, this step is not sufficient, since it can lead to deadlocks.

DEFINITION 6.5.– Deadlock – *A deadlock occurs when at least two partitions need to grow and there is no free node left in the infrastructure.*

6.1.4.2. *Overview of deadlock management*

To avoid deadlocks, our approach consists of merging partitions by pairs. Merging two partitions does not guarantee that the corresponding events can be solved; however, it provides the scheduler with more opportunities to migrate VMs. This is even more true if two complementary events are involved, for instance an "overloaded node" event and "underloaded node" event.

To identify partitions that could benefit from a merge, we associate a state with each partition: created, growing, blocked or destroyed (see Figure 6.4).

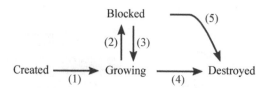

(1) A node generates an event, its processing starts
(2) The event traverses the ring without being solved
(3) At least one new node joins the partition
(4) The event is solved
(5) No solution can be found, the event is dropped

Figure 6.4. *States associated with a partition*

When a partition is created, its initial state is set to *growing*. It keeps this state until the corresponding event comes back to its initiator; when it occurs, the partition is then identified as *blocked*. It does not necessarily mean that there is no free node left, but this is a possibility.

The event continues to traverse the ring while it is not solved and there remains at least one node on the outside of the associated partition P_1; to speed up this procedure, we use the shortcuts presented previously. When the event arrives on a node on the outside of P_1, there are three possibilities:

1) The node belongs to a *growing* partition P_2; the event is then forwarded to the first node on the outside of P_2; it would indeed be irrelevant to merge P_1 and P_2 since P_2 may be able to solve its event by itself and would then be negatively impacted if it had to absorb more nodes than required.

2) The node belongs to a *blocked* partition P_2; the two partitions then try to merge with each other; if they do not succeed, the event is forwarded to the first node on the outside of P_2; if they do succeed, the resulting partition switches to *growing*. We will return to partition merging later.

3) The node is free; it then joins partition P_1, which switches to *growing*.

If a solution is found, the processing procedure ends with success; on the contrary, if all nodes in the infrastructure belong to the same partition and no solution is found, it guarantees that the problem is unsolvable.

The steps of the deadlock management algorithm are summarized in Figure 6.5.

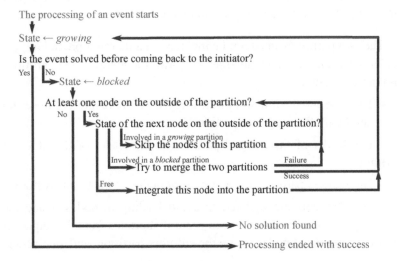

Figure 6.5. *Deadlock management algorithm*

6.1.4.3. *Details on the partition merging algorithm*

As promised, we give here more details on the merge of two partitions.

First, we need to make a distinction between requester partition and the enforcer partition.

DEFINITION 6.6.– Requester partition – *The requester partition is the partition that requests for the merge.*

DEFINITION 6.7.– Enforcer partition – *The enforcer partition is the partition that enforces the merge.*

To avoid the situation where the two partitions try to take the requester role at the same time, we define a total ordering by associating a unique identifier with each node, depending on its location on the ring; we arbitrarily chose that the partition whose leader has the lower identifier would be the requester.

The two partitions must not be involved in a merging procedure; the leader of the enforcer partition then performs the merge of the partitions and the associated events:

– The type and the initiator of the merged event are those of the event associated with the requester partition.

– The leader of the merged partition is the leader of the enforcer partition.

– The merged partition is composed of nodes of the two partitions.

– The shortcuts are updated to avoid leading to nodes inside the merged partition; this situation can occur if shortcuts from the requester partition referenced nodes inside the enforcer partition, and vice versa.

Once the partitions are merged, the new leader starts a scheduling computation to try to solve the merged event.

Consider an example involving three partitions (see Figure 6.6) to summarize the concepts presented so far to manage deadlocks. Partitions P_1 and P_3 are initially *blocked* (see Figure 6.6(a)); the identifier of the leader of P_1, 6, is lower than the one of the leader of P_3, 8; therefore, P_1 is the requester and P_3 the enforcer; the merged partition has the same color as the requester, to recall the type of the event (see Figure 6.6(b)). If the two remaining partitions are also *blocked*, the merging procedure is again applied; this time, P_2 is the requester and P_1 is the enforcer; the merged partition has the same color as P_2, to recall the type of the event (see Figure 6.6(c)). If a scheduling computation on the merged partition cannot solve the associated event, we then have the guarantee that no solution existed, since all the nodes in the infrastructure were considered.

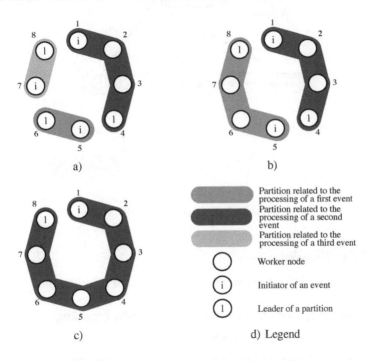

a)

b)

c)

d) Legend

Partition related to the processing of a first event
Partition related to the processing of a second event
Partition related to the processing of a third event
Worker node
Initiator of an event
Leader of a partition

Figure 6.6. *Merging partitions to avoid deadlocks*

6.2. Implementation

The concepts presented so far were implemented in a prototype written in Java.

The prototype was able to handle "overloaded node" and "underloaded node" events.

6.2.1. *Architecture of an agent*

The prototype was deployed as a set of software agents, each agent being in charge of managing one node; each DVMS agent was made of five main components: a knowledge base, an observer, a client, a server and a scheduler (see Figure 6.7).

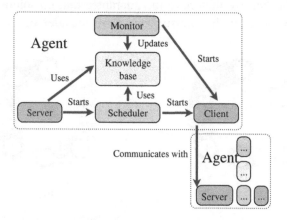

Figure 6.7. *Architecture of a DVMS agent*

6.2.1.1. *Knowledge base*

The knowledge base stores several pieces of information.

Some information is available continuously, regarding:

– the resources of the node;

– the VMs hosted by this node, and their consumption of resources;

– overload and underload thresholds;

– the internet protocol (IP) address and the port to contact the agent on the neighbor node.

Other information is available only during the processing of an event, regarding:

– the initiator;

– the current leader of the partition;

– the shortcut (IP address and port number) to contact the agent of the first node on the outside of the partition;

– the state of the partition.

In addition, the leader of the partition has some information on the resources of each node involved in the partition.

6.2.1.2. *Observer*

The observer periodically (by default, every two seconds) updates the content of the knowledge base regarding the VMs hosted on the node and their consumption of resources.

If it detects a problem and the node is not already involved in a partition, it generates an event, reserves the node to solve this event and forwards the latter to the agent on the neighbor node by means of a client.

6.2.1.3. *Client*

A client is started each time a message has to be sent to the agent on another node.

A message is a Java object that is transferred to a server by means of a socket.

6.2.1.4. *Server*

A server processes incoming messages.

In the case of an initiator, it may have to check that the event is still valid.

In the case of a leader, it manages merge requests coming from other partitions.

In the case of any other node, it:

– handles the requests to reserve or free the node;

– updates the knowledge base, in case of a leader change, with information related to (1) the new leader, (2) the agent of the first node on the outside of the partition and (3) the state of the partition;

– sends information on request of the leader regarding the VMs hosted by the node and their consumption of resources;

– updates the knowledge base, in case of a migration, regarding the list of VMs hosted by the node;

– decides on what to do when it receives an event, either to forward it to the agent of the first node on the outside of the partition, or to launch a scheduler to try to solve the event.

6.2.1.5. *Scheduler*

A scheduler first checks that the event it tries to solve is still valid; it contacts the initiator for this purpose.

If the event is not valid anymore, the scheduler destroys the partition to free the nodes.

On the contrary, if the event is still valid, the scheduler tries to compute a reconfiguration plan. For this purpose, it leverages the scheduling algorithms of an external scheduler; during our experiments, we used the algorithms that were originally designed for the Entropy manager (we will come back to this later); however, it could use other algorithms.

If the scheduler does not find a reconfiguration plan, it forwards the event to the agent of the first node on the outside of the partition.

If the scheduler finds a plan, it applies it once the event is solved, the scheduler destroys the partition.

6.2.2. *Leveraging the scheduling algorithms designed for entropy*

Entropy [HER 09, HER 10, HER 11] is a centralized and autonomous manager that can dynamically schedule VMs in a data center.

Entropy relies on constraint programming to compute a reconfiguration plan, which presents several advantages. This enables us to find an optimal solution, or a solution that is close to the optimal solution, depending on the time that is allocated to the computing of a reconfiguration plan. Moreover, it is possible to define generic scheduling algorithms and add as many constraints as necessary, for instance on the placement of VMs, without requiring the modification of the algorithm on each addition.

Entropy has several characteristics that are particularly interesting in the context of this work. First, Entropy implements several scheduling algorithms that are dedicated to VMs; the first version of Entropy is better known for its consolidation algorithm [HER 09], while the second version focuses on solving constraint violations and provides a better scalability [HER 11]. Moreover, Entropy tries to minimize the number of virtual machine migrations, given that they are costly. In addition, Entropy is able to manage *vjobs*, in other words groups of interdependent VMs [HER 10]. Entropy also enables us to define placement constraints related to affinities or antagonisms between VMs. Furthermore, Entropy quickly discovers if there is no solution, which is a good thing for the DVMS event processing procedure. Finally, Entropy is written in Java, which facilitates its integration into DVMS.

6.3. Conclusion

In this chapter, we detailed our decentralized approach, distributed virtual machine scheduler (DVMS), to dynamically schedule VMs in data centers.

We first presented the fundamental concepts behind DVMS [QUE 12]: the distribution of the scheduling work over software agents installed on each node and organized following a ring topology, the triggering of a scheduling procedure when an event occurs on the infrastructure, and the dynamic partitioning of the infrastructure to avoid conflicts between schedulers, without requiring a single service node.

We then proposed two improvements on the algorithm in charge of processing events [QUE 13]. The first improvement enables us to speed up the traversal of the ring, by defining on each node of a partition an ever up-to-date shortcut that leads to the first node on the outside of this partition. The second improvement consists of guaranteeing that an event will always be solved if a solution exists; to handle deadlocks, we proposed to merge partitions by pairs; this provides the scheduler working on the merged partition with more opportunities to migrate VMs.

After that, we explained how we implemented these concepts in a prototype written in Java. We mentioned that DVMS could leverage several scheduling algorithms to compute a reconfiguration plan for each partition. In the context of this work, we chose to use those designed for Entropy [HER 09, HER 10, HER 11], a centralized VM manager.

In the following, we will see that DVMS was validated by means of experiments. We will finally study its limits and perspectives.

7

Experimental Protocol and Testing Environment

In the previous chapter, we detailed the concepts behind the distributed virtual machine scheduler (DVMS) and its implementation; in this chapter, we will present the methodology and the tools we used to validate DVMS.

First, we will describe the experimental protocol. Then, we will focus on the framework we developed to test DVMS by means of simulations and experiments on the Grid'5000 test bed [GRI 13]. Finally, we will see how we used the SimGrid toolkit [CAS 08] to overcome the limitations of the testing framework.

7.1. Experimental protocol

We defined an experimental protocol to evaluate DVMS.

7.1.1. *Choosing a testing platform*

First, we chose the platform to perform the experiments. This platform could be a real one (Grid'5000) or a simulated one (when we used the SimGrid toolkit).

7.1.2. *Defining the experimental parameters*

Then, we defined the experimental parameters.

We chose the number of nodes to use and their resource capacities. We considered only CPU and memory, but it would be interesting to add networks and disks as well.

We specified the number of virtual machines (VMs) and their maximum demand for resources. Once again, we considered only CPU and memory.

Note that the number of nodes and VMs remained constant during each of our experiments.

7.1.3. *Initializing the experiment*

Subsequently, we initialized the experiment.

In case of a real platform, we configured the nodes before creating the VMs.

In all cases, we configured and started the scheduler we wanted to evaluate, i.e. either DVMS or Entropy [HER 09, HER 10, HER 11], keeping in mind that we aimed at comparing them.

7.1.4. *Injecting a workload*

Afterward, we injected a CPU workload into each VM to observe the behavior of each scheduler.

The workload could be computed using a random function (reproducibility is guaranteed by means of a seed) or by reading a trace file.

In the case of a real experiment on Grid'5000, we injected the workload. However, in any other case, we simulated the injection.

We spread load injection over time for the simulations with SimGrid (see Figure 7.1(a)); therefore, the workload was likely to vary while the scheduler optimized the placement of VMs; this mimicked the behavior of a real system. In any other case, using the testing framework, the load remained constant while a scheduler was working (see Figure 7.1(b)); the goal was then to observe the ability of the scheduler to solve a given set of problems.

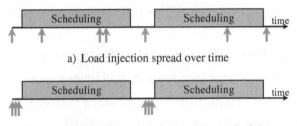

a) Load injection spread over time

b) Load injection done before launching a scheduler

Figure 7.1. *Different types of load injection*

7.1.5. *Processing results*

When the experiment was over, we collected the results and processed them by means of a statistical analysis script written in R.

7.2. Testing framework

As mentioned before, we developed a framework in Java to evaluate the DVMS prototype from the early stages of its design and implementation.

This framework mainly enables us to deploy DVMS agents, inject the workload and collect experimental results.

7.2.1. *Configuration*

This framework was configurable. The user could especially specify:

– the type of the experiment, either simulation or experiment on a real system;

– the number of nodes;

– the number of VMs to create, and their maximum demand for CPU and memory resources;

– the number of different values a VM CPU consumption can take;

– the number of changes in VM CPU consumption during a single experiment;

– the way to retrieve the CPU workload to be injected into each VM:

- by means of a file specifying the CPU consumption of each VM;

- by means of a function that computes a random CPU workload for each VM; a seed was used to ensure reproducibility.

In case of a simulation, it was also necessary to specify the number of nodes to simulate and their CPU and memory capacities.

7.2.2. *Components*

The testing framework was made up of three main components: a knowledge base, a server and a driver, see Figure 7.2.

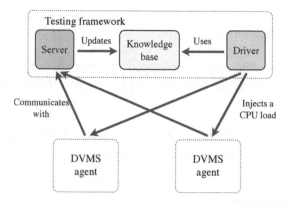

Figure 7.2. *Architecture of the testing framework*

7.2.2.1. *Knowledge base*

The knowledge base stored:

– the parameters specified by the user, which were presented previously;

– the CPU and memory capacities of each node;

– the CPU and memory consumptions of each VM;

– the list of VMs hosted by a node;

– whether or not agents were allowed to generate a new event;

– the list of events that were being processed.

7.2.2.2. *Server*

The server-processed messages sent by DVMS agents to inform that:

– a new agent was operational;

– a new partition was being created;

– a partition had been destroyed;

– an "overloaded node" event had been solved.

7.2.2.3. *Driver*

The driver drove the experiment.

At the beginning of the experiment, the driver:

1) decided, in a round-robin way, which node each VM was assigned to;

2) created the VMs, in case of an experiment on a real infrastructure;

3) decided, in a round-robin way, which node each DVMS agent was assigned to;

4) launched the DVMS agents;

5) waited until all DVMS agents were operational.

Then, the driver repeated the same sequence of instructions while the experiment was running and:

1) computed or retrieved the new value of the CPU consumption for each VM;

2) notified each node about the new CPU consumption for each VM this node hosted;

3) injected the workload into each VM, in case of an experiment on a real infrastructure;

4) allowed DVMS agents to generate new events;

5) waited until all "overloaded node" events were solved;

6) forbade DVMS agents to generate new events;

7) waited until all partitions were destroyed;

8) wrote data into a structured text file regarding:

- the number of events that were generated,

- the time elapsed between the load injection and the resolution of all problems,

- the number of nodes that hosted at least one VM.

Finally, at the end of the experiment, the driver:

1) Collected files written by DVMS agent, that contained data on each scheduling procedure that occurred:

- the event that was processed,

- the number of nodes that were involved in the partition,

- the result of the scheduling procedure, success or failure,

- the time to compute a reconfiguration plan,

- the time to apply the reconfiguration plan.

2) Concatenated the results into a structured text file.

A statistical analysis script written in R then processed the results.

A similar testing framework was implemented to drive Entropy, keeping in mind that we wanted to compare its behavior with that of the DVMS.

7.3. Grid'5000 test bed

We used the Grid'5000 test bed to deploy DVMS along the testing framework, to perform simulations and real experiments.

7.3.1. *Presentation*

Grid'5000 is "a scientific instrument supporting experiment-driven research in all areas of computer science, including high performance computing, distributed computing, networking and big data" [GRI 13].

At the time of this work, the Grid'5000 test bed was composed of 10 sites (each site is equivalent to a data center), including nine located in France and one in Luxembourg. It comprised of 25 clusters and almost 1,200 nodes with various characteristics regarding CPU, memory, storage and network.

7.3.2. *Simulations*

We first used Grid'5000 to evaluate DVMS by means of simulations.

Before performing a simulation, we had to:

1) reserve nodes, using oarsub [CAP 05];

2) deploy a Linux Debian distribution on each node, by means of kadeploy3 [KAD 13];

3) install the software stack used for the simulations:

- the testing framework and Entropy, on a service node,

- DVMS, on each worker node,

- the Java runtime environment (JRE), on each node, to run the programs mentioned previously, that were written in Java,

- Network time protocol (NTP), to synchronize time among nodes,

- sentinelle.pl, a script that allowed us to quickly run a given command on a great deal of nodes,

- Taktuk [TAK 13], to quickly exchange files between the service node and the worker ones.

4) configure the DVMS agents and the testing framework;

5) synchronize the clock of all nodes, by means of ntpdate.

We could then start a simulation before collecting the results.

The biggest simulation we performed on Grid'5000 involved 65,536 simulated VMs and 10,240 DVMS agents that were distributed across 28 nodes from the Suno cluster, which was located on the Sophia site.

7.3.3. *Real experiments*

Once the DVMS prototype was more mature, we evaluated it by means of real experiments, as opposed to simulations, on Grid'5000.

The real experiment preparation step was similar to the simulated one, even if it implied, in addition, to:

1) reserve, using oarsub, a global virtual local area networks (VLAN) and a range of IP addresses, to enable network communications with VMs;

2) install a hypervisor on each worker node, to create VMs; we chose KVM [KIV 07];

3) install Libvirt [LIB 13] on each worker node, to facilitate the use of KVM;

4) copy, by means of Taktuk, a VM disk image template on each worker node; this disk image was shared between all VMs hosted on the same node; it was read-only, and the modifications performed by each VM were stored in dedicated files; when a VM was migrated, the corresponding file was automatically transferred by KVM;

5) create each VM and configure its network interface, using Libvirt.

These preliminary operations were performed by the Flauncher tool [BAL 12], which was designed in the context of the Hemera initiative [HEM 13].

During an experiment, the testing framework had to:

– inject a real workload into each VM, using stress;

– migrate VMs, using Libvirt, when it applied a reconfiguration plan.

The biggest experiment we performed involved 4,754 VMs and 467 nodes distributed across four sites (Nancy, Rennes, Sophia and

Toulouse) and eight clusters. The routing of network communications was performed by KaVLAN [KAV 13].

7.4. SimGrid simulation toolkit

We used the SimGrid toolkit [CAS 08] to complement the experiments performed on Grid'5000.

7.4.1. *Presentation*

SimGrid is "a scientific instrument to study the behavior of large-scale distributed systems such as Grids, Clouds, HPC or P2P systems" [SIM 13].

SimGrid includes four application programming interfaces (API) to implement distributed applications:

1) SMPI is used to run unmodified Message Passing Interface (MPI) programs; it only requires recompiling these programs;

2) SimDag is used for bags of tasks modeled by means of a direct acyclic graph;

3) Grid reality and simulation (GRAS) allows users to develop programs for grids; there are two implementations of this interface; the first one is used to simulate the behavior of grid programs, whereas the second one enables us to deploy them on a real infrastructure;

4) MSG is a simplified interface used to simulate applications composed of several concurrent processes.

7.4.2. *Port of DVMS to SimGrid*

The MSG API was the best suited one for DVMS; however, to use it, we had to apply several modifications to DVMS and the testing framework to:

– transform Java threads into SimGrid processes;

– replace network communications performed with sockets by task exchanges using SimGrid mailboxes;

– avoid relying on Java synchronization primitives, since they could interfere with SimGrid; moreover, SimGrid ensured there were no concurrent operations;

– instrument the code to measure the passage of simulation time;

– instrument the code to get traces.

We also rewrote the load injection function to spread injection over time.

7.4.3. *Advantages compared to the simulations on Grid'5000*

Despite the modifications applied to DVMS and to the testing framework to port them on SimGrid, this toolkit offered several advantages. SimGrid could indeed:

– simulate bigger infrastructures;

– avoid problems linked with distributed systems, like the necessity to synchronize time on all nodes or to handle node failures;

– spread the workload injection over time;

– generate traces that could be imported in a visualization tool like Paje [PAJ 13]; this was more readable than log files generated by DVMS; besides, it enabled us to detect and correct bugs;

– improve the reproducibility of experiments; for example, the scheduling of DVMS agents did not depend on the Linux scheduler anymore.

7.4.4. *Simulations*

Performing a simulation with SimGrid first required us to:

1) configure the DVMS agents and the testing framework;

2) describe the infrastructure to be simulated; we chose to model it as a cluster with full routing between nodes;

3) describe the deployment; the deployment file was automatically generated and was used to specify (1) that the arguments passed to each DVMS agent, (2) that an agent had to be deployed on each worker node

and (3) that the testing framework had to be deployed on the service node.

We then started the simulation before collecting the traces and processing them with Paje.

The biggest simulation we performed involved 150,000 VMs and 10,000 nodes. The CPU consumption of each VM was modified every 2 min; the simulation time was equal to 1 h.

7.5. Conclusion

In this chapter, we have presented our methodology and the tools that we used to validate DVMS.

We first focused on the experimental protocol.

We then mentioned that we implemented a testing framework to evaluate DVMS and explained how it worked and how to configure it.

We also described the deployment of this framework on the Grid'5000 test bed [GRI 13], to evaluate DVMS by means of simulations and real experiments.

Finally, we showed how the SimGrid toolkit [CAS 08] helped us with simulations.

In the next chapter, we will focus on analyzing the results obtained during the experiments.

8

Experimental Results and Validation of DVMS

To validate the distributed virtual machine scheduler (DVMS), we compared it with the centralized version of Entropy [HER 09, HER 11].

The first version of Entropy aimed at consolidating virtual machines (VMs) on a limited number of nodes, while the second version focused on repairing the infrastructure by correcting node overload problems and placement constraint violations. Even though this strategy change enabled us to significantly reduce the computation time of a reconfiguration plan [HER 11], Entropy still considered all problems at once, therefore impacting the scalability of this approach.

To evaluate how DVMS enabled us to improve the scalability and reactivity of the scheduling policies designed for Entropy, we performed several experiments with the two frameworks by leveraging the experimental protocol and the testing environment defined in the previous chapter. First, we performed simulations on the Grid'5000 test bed [GRI 13]; then, we tested DVMS and Entropy with real VMs, again on Grid'5000; finally, we conducted simulations with the SimGrid toolkit [CAS 08].

In this chapter, we present the results of the experiments we carried out with DVMS and Entropy.

8.1. Simulations on Grid'5000

We performed two sets of simulations on Grid'5000 to compare Entropy and DVMS.

The first set leveraged the consolidation algorithm designed for Entropy 1, while the second set was done with the repair algorithm designed for Entropy 2.

We ensured that, at each step of each simulation, Entropy and DVMS worked on the same initial configuration; in other words, the VMs were initially placed on the same nodes, and the loads injected into the VMs were identical, so that Entropy and DVMS had to solve the same problems.

We used several criteria to compare Entropy and DVMS. The first criterion was the length of an iteration, in other words the time elapsed between the end of the load injection and the end of the last solving procedure; note that only the time to compute reconfiguration plans had an influence on this length, since we considered that their application was instantaneous during these simulations. Another criterion was the size of a partition, in other words the number of nodes that were required to solve a problem. A third criterion was the cost of a reconfiguration plan, to estimate the time to apply such a plan; this information was available only for the first set of simulations, since Entropy 2 relied on a cost model that did not allow us to compare Entropy and DVMS; because DVMS tried to limit the size of each partition, we supposed that its behavior would be the same for the two sets of simulations.

For each set of simulations, we detail the experimental parameters before presenting and analyzing the results.

8.1.1. *Consolidation*

8.1.1.1. *Experimental parameters*

We performed the first set of simulations with the consolidation algorithm designed for Entropy 1 on a HP Proliant DL165 G7 node, which had two processors (AMD Opteron 6164 HE and 12 cores, 1.7 GHz) and 48 GB of memory.

Our software stack was composed of a Linux Debian 6 (Squeeze) 64 bits distribution, OpenJDK JRE 6 and Entropy 1.1.1.

The simulations involved infrastructures composed of (1) 128 VMs distributed across 64 nodes, and (2) 256 VMs distributed across 128 nodes; we could not simulate bigger infrastructures, since Entropy 1 could not handle it.

Each simulation was performed over 30 iterations.

The simulated nodes had two processors running at 2 GHz, and 4 GB of memory. The simulated VMs had one virtual processor running at 2 GHz, and 1 GB of memory. A VM could consume 0, 400, 800, 1,200, 1,600 or 2,000 GHz.

We configured DVMS to detect that a node was:

– overloaded if its VMs tried to consume more than 100% of its processor or memory resources;

– underloaded if either the processor consumption was below 20% or the memory consumption was below 50%.

We also configured DVMS and Entropy so that the number of seconds to compute a reconfiguration plan was, at worse, equal to four times the number of nodes considered during the computation. Note that we determined this value empirically.

8.1.1.2. *Results*

Figures 8.1, 8.2, 8.3, 8.4, 8.5 and 8.6 present the trends of the main evaluation criteria through a graphical representation of the average and standard deviation of the values we obtained.

The average number of events injected at each iteration can be seen in Figure 8.1.

We can first observe in Figure 8.2 that DVMS was, up to five times on average, as fast as Entropy to solve all problems.

The speed of DVMS did not significantly impact the consolidation rate, since DVMS used on average only two or three additional nodes to host all VMs (see Figure 8.3). However, this result was obtained by specifying a relatively high underload threshold; a node could be identified as underloaded even if it was not, in reality, and it could take time to find enough nodes to host all of its VMs.

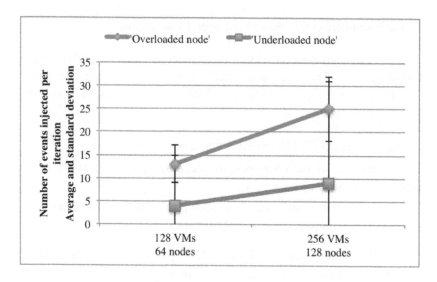

Figure 8.1. *Average number of events injected per iteration*
with the consolidation algorithm

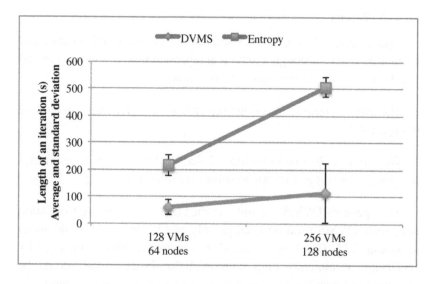

Figure 8.2. *Average length of an iteration with the consolidation algorithm*

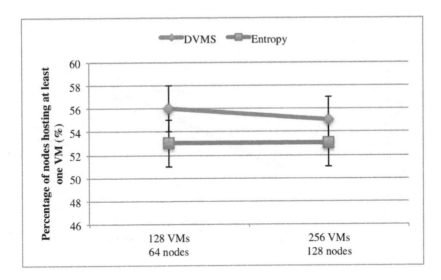

Figure 8.3. *Average percentage of nodes hosting at least
one VM with the consolidation algorithm*

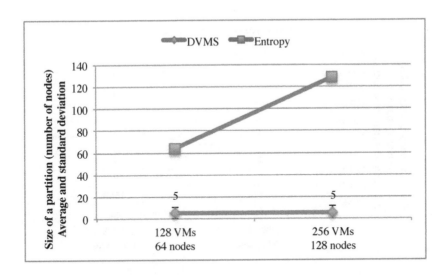

Figure 8.4. *Average size of a partition with the consolidation algorithm*

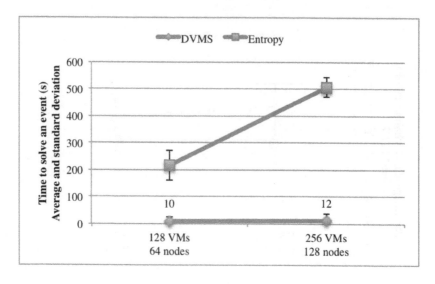

Figure 8.5. *Average time to solve an event with the consolidation algorithm*

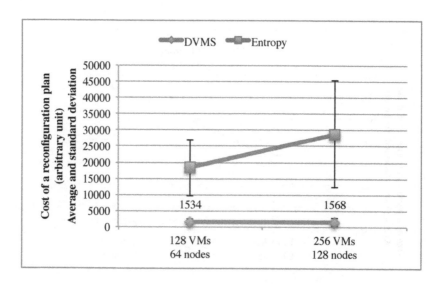

Figure 8.6. *Average cost of applying a reconfiguration plan with the consolidation algorithm*

Now, consider the results on a partition scale, and no longer on an infrastructure scale; we can observe in Figure 8.4 that DVMS built small partitions to solve the problems, involving five nodes on average, and only three nodes on average if we consider only the "overloaded node" problems. However, Entropy considered all nodes of the infrastructure to compute each reconfiguration plan.

The smaller the partition was, the lower the time to solve an event was (see Figure 8.5). Note that Entropy solved all problems at once, which explains why the time to solve an event was equal to the corresponding iteration length; this was true only because we considered that reconfiguration plans were applied instantaneously.

Besides impacting the time to solve an event, the size of a partition influenced the cost of the corresponding reconfiguration plan: the smaller the partition was, the cheaper the reconfiguration plan was (see Figure 8.6); we can explain this by considering that, the smaller the partition was, the fewer VM migrations there were. However, it is necessary to moderate this observation: an Entropy reconfiguration plan allowed us to solve all problems at once; therefore, the cost to apply all DVMS reconfiguration plans could be higher than the cost of an Entropy plan; nevertheless, we focused with DVMS on accelerating the solving procedure as much as possible, this is why we did not consider the total cost but the cost associated with each problem.

8.1.2. *Infrastructure repair*

To improve the scalability, a more recent version of Entropy [HER 11] was designed to maintain the viability of the infrastructure, by periodically monitoring the resources consumed by the VMs and checking the placement constraints specified by the administrator.

The repair algorithm designed for Entropy 2 did not try to consolidate the VMs on a restricted set of nodes; in other words, it did not do anything in case a node was underloaded. That is why we disabled the generation of "underloaded node" events in DVMS.

8.1.2.1. *Experimental parameters*

We performed the second set of simulations with the repair algorithm designed for Entropy 2 on 3, 6 and 12 (respectively, for the simulation of 2,048 VMs and 320 nodes, 4,096 VMs and 640 nodes and 8,192 VMs and 1,280 nodes) on HP Proliant DL165 G7 nodes that had two processors (AMD Opteron 6164 HE, 12 cores, 1.7 GHz) and 48 GB of memory.

Our software stack was composed of a Linux Debian 6 (Squeeze) 64 bits distribution, OpenJDK JRE 6 and Entropy 2.1.

Each simulation was performed over 30 iterations.

The simulated nodes had four processors (five arbitrary units of capacity each) and 8 GB of memory. The simulated VMs had one virtual processor and 1 GB of memory. The processor consumption of a VM could be equal to 0, 1, 2, 3, 4 or 5 arbitrary units.

We configured DVMS to consider that a node was overloaded if its VMs tried to consume more than 100% of its processor or memory resources. We disabled the generation of "underloaded node" events, as mentioned previously.

We also configured DVMS and Entropy so that the number of seconds to compute the reconfiguration plan was, at worse, equal to one-tenth the number of nodes considered during the computation. Note that we determined this value empirically.

8.1.2.2. *Results*

Figures 8.7, 8.8, 8.9 and 8.10 present the trends for the main evaluation criteria through a graphical representation of the average and standard deviation for the values we obtained. Note that the error bars are not always visible, since the standard deviation values are relatively low.

The average number of events injected during each iteration is visible in Figure 8.7.

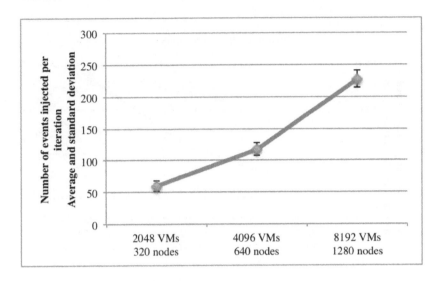

Figure 8.7. *Average number of events injected per iteration with the repair algorithm*

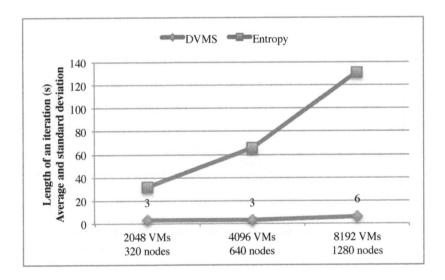

Figure 8.8. *Average length of an iteration with the repair algorithm*

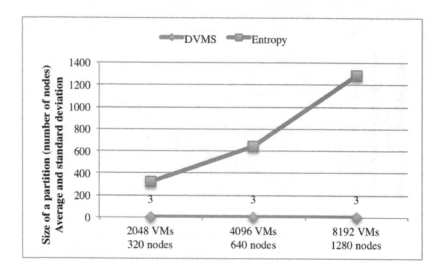

Figure 8.9. *Average size of a partition with the repair algorithm*

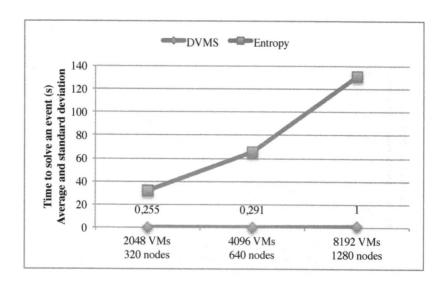

Figure 8.10. *Average time to solve an event with the repair algorithm*

Figure 8.8 presents the average iteration length. We first observe a dramatic decrease, compared to the results obtained with the consolidation algorithm, even though the simulated infrastructure was much bigger, since there were up to 10 times as many nodes and 32 times as many VMs. We also notice that DVMS was up to 10 to 20 times as fast as Entropy to solve all problems.

Note that each node of the infrastructure always hosted several VMs, since the repair algorithm did not aim at consolidating VMs. Therefore, the percentage of nodes hosting at least one VM was not relevant.

The average size of a partition remained very low (see Figure 8.9): three nodes, the same as for the consolidation algorithm.

We can again observe that the time to solve a problem (see 8.10) depended on the size of the corresponding partition.

Moreover, we notice that DVMS behaved particularly well with the repair algorithm and without the "underloaded node" events, since the time to solve an event was below 1 s, on average.

8.2. Real experiments on Grid'5000

Performing simulations on Grid'5000 was interesting, since we obtained useful information regarding the behavior of DVMS and its advantages compared to Entropy. However, it did not enable us to study the cost of applying reconfiguration plans.

Therefore, to complete our evaluation, we compared Entropy and DVMS by means of real experiments on Grid'5000.

8.2.1. *Experimental parameters*

We performed the real experiments with the repair algorithm designed for Entropy 2.

The number and characteristics of the worker nodes we used can be seen, respectively, in Figure 8.11 and Table 8.1. The service node belonged to the Suno cluster.

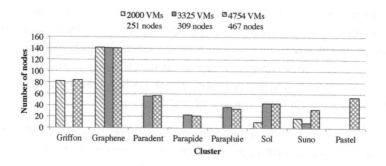

Figure 8.11. *Worker nodes used for the real experiments*

Site	Cluster	Processor	RAM (GB)
Nancy	Griffon	Intel; 2x4 cores; 2.50 GHz	16
	Graphene	Intel; 1x4 cores; 2.60 GHz	16
Rennes	Paradent	Intel; 2x4 cores; 2.50 GHz	32
	Parapide	Intel; 2x4 cores; 2.93 GHz	24
	Parapluie	AMD; 2x12 cores; 1.70 GHz	48
Sophia	Sol	AMD; 2x2 cores; 2.60 GHz	4
	Suno	Intel; 2x4 cores; 2.26 GHz	32
Toulouse	Pastel	AMD; 2x2 cores; 2.61 GHz	8

Table 8.1. *Characteristics of the nodes used for the real experiments*

Our software stack was composed of a Linux Debian 6 (Squeeze) 64 bits distribution, OpenJDK JRE 6, virt-install 0.600.1, virsh 0.9.12, KVM 1.1.2, Flauncher and Entropy 2.1.

Each experiment was performed over 10 iterations.

Each VM had one virtual processor and 1 GB of memory. A VM could consume either 0% or 100% of its virtual processor.

We configured DVMS to consider that a node was overloaded if its VMs tried to consume more than 100% of its processor or memory resources. We disabled the generation of "underloaded node" events.

We also configured DVMS and Entropy so that the number of seconds to compute the reconfiguration plan was, at worse, equal to one-tenth the number of nodes considered during the computation. Recall that we determined this value empirically.

8.2.2. Results

Figures 8.12, 8.13, 8.14 and 8.15 present the trends of the main evaluation criteria through a graphical representation of the average and standard deviation of the values we obtained.

The average number of problems injected during each iteration can be seen in Figure 8.12.

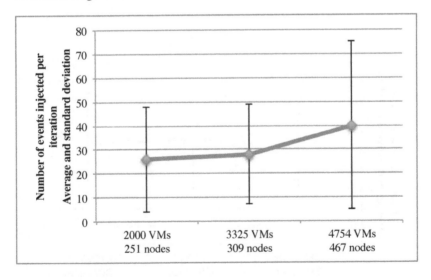

Figure 8.12. *Average number of events injected per iteration with the repair algorithm*

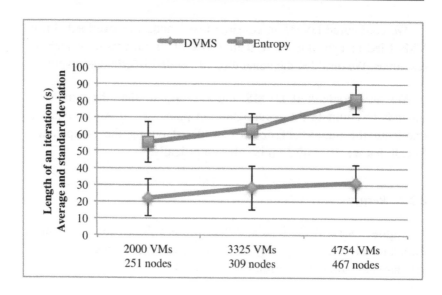

Figure 8.13. *Average length of an iteration with the repair algorithm*

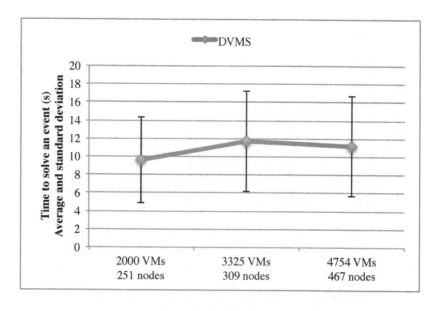

Figure 8.14. *Average time to solve an event with the repair algorithm*

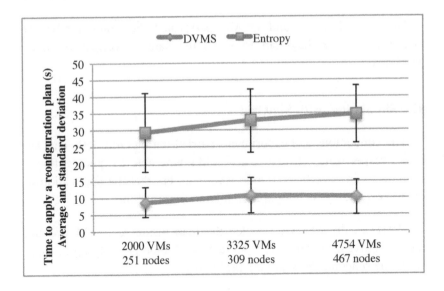

Figure 8.15. *Average time to apply a reconfiguration plan*
with the repair algorithm

We can first observe that the average iteration length (see Figure 8.13) was much longer than during the simulations. This is true for DVMS as well as Entropy. In fact, if the absolute gap between DVMS and Entropy remained the same, the relative gap decreased.

In the case of DVMS, the rise of the iteration length can be explained by the rise of the time required to solve each problem (see Figure 8.14). In fact, while DVMS solved "overloaded node" problems in less than 1 s on average during the simulations, it took more than 10 s during the real experiments.

If DVMS spent more time solving each event, it was because applying the reconfiguration plans took time (see Figure 8.15). In fact, in the case of DVMS, the time to solve an event if largely dominated by the time to apply the reconfiguration plan, since the time to compute a plan is low, as showed during the simulations. However, Entropy spent roughly as much time computing a reconfiguration plan as applying it.

Note that Entropy and DVMS performed the same number of migrations, since they had to solve the same "overloaded node" problems.

8.3. Simulations with SimGrid

The simulations and experiments carried out on Grid'5000 enabled us to, respectively, observe that DVMS was able to quickly find a solution to an "overloaded node" problem, but that the application of the corresponding reconfiguration plan took some time.

However, the way we injected the load inside each VM was not representative of a real system; in fact, we avoided modifying the load while the scheduler was solving problems.

Therefore, to complete our evaluation of DVMS and Entropy, we performed other simulations with the SimGrid toolkit by spreading the load injection over time.

8.3.1. *Experimental parameters*

We performed each SimGrid simulation with the repair algorithm designed for Entropy 2 on an HP Proliant DL165 G7 node that had two processors (AMD Opteron 6164 HE, 12 cores, 1.7 GHz) and 48 GB of memory.

Our software stack was composed of a Linux Debian 6 (Squeeze) 64 bits distribution, OpenJDK JRE 6, SimGrid 3.7.1 and Entropy 2.1.

The simulations involved infrastructures composed of:
- 5,120 VMs and 512 nodes;
- 10,240 VMs and 1,024 nodes;
- 20,480 VMs and 2,048 nodes;
- 40,960 VMs and 4,096 nodes;
- 81,920 VMs and 8,192 nodes.

The simulated duration of each experiment was set to 1 h.

The simulated nodes had 8 processors with a capacity of 100 arbitrary units each, and 20 GB of memory. The simulated VMs had one virtual processor and 1 GB of memory. The processor consumption of a VM could be equal to 0, 10, 20, 30, 40, 50, 60, 70, 80, 90 or 100 arbitrary units. The processor consumption of a VM followed an exponential law with an expected value and a standard deviation of 50 arbitrary units; therefore, in steady state, the VMs consumed 50 arbitrary units of processor on average; consequently, the overall processor consumption was equal to 62.5% of the infrastructure processor capacity. The processor consumption of each VM changed every 5 minutes, on average.

We configured DVMS to consider that a node was overloaded if its VMs tried to consume more than 100% of its processor or memory resources. We disabled the generation of "underloaded node" events.

DVMS monitored the resources of each node every second. Entropy was first configured to wait 1 s at the end of a scheduling computation before starting a new one; this delay was then set to 30 seconds.

We configured DVMS and Entropy so that the number of seconds to compute a reconfiguration plan was equal, at worse, to one-fourth of the number of nodes considered during the computation. Note that, like for the simulations on Grid'5000, we considered that the reconfiguration plans were applied instantaneously.

8.3.2. *Results*

Figure 8.16 presents the cumulated computation time for DVMS and Entropy. We can see on this figure that Entropy spent a lot of time computing reconfiguration plans; in fact, when the size of the infrastructure was increased, it worked almost all the time. Apparently, DVMS spent much time computing reconfiguration plans; however, if we divide this time by the number of nodes, we can see that it is in fact very low, a few tenths of seconds on average per node for one hour of simulation.

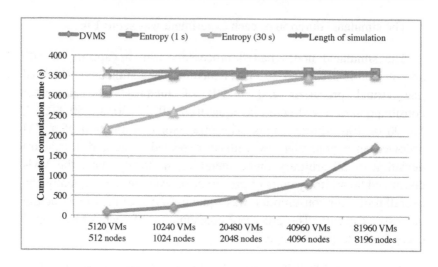

Figure 8.16. *Cumulated computation time*

We already knew that DVMS reacted quickly to solve "overloaded node" problems; this is confirmed by Figure 8.17. In fact, the cumulated overload time for 1 h of simulation was roughly equal to 12 min for DVMS; in other words, each node was overloaded by less than one-tenth of a second on average. However, we must not forget that the reconfiguration plans were applied instantaneously.

Figure 8.17 also presents a surprising result: Entropy had no apparent positive effect with the experimental parameters we used. It seems that the VM resource consumptions fluctuated during the computation of reconfiguration plans; therefore, these plans were outdated and inefficient.

8.4. Conclusion

In this chapter, we studied the experimental results obtained during the evaluation of Entropy [HER 09, HER 11] and DVMS.

By analyzing the results of the simulations performed on the Grid'5000 test bed, we observed that DVMS usually built small partitions, which allowed it to quickly find a solution to "overloaded node" and "underloaded node" problems. Moreover, the speed of

DVMS had no significant negative impact on the consolidation rate, since DVMS behaved well compared to Entropy.

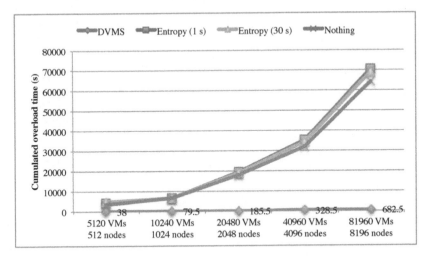

Figure 8.17. *Cumulated overload time*

Then, we completed these evaluations by performing real experiments on Grid'5000 [GRI 13], to observe the cost of applying reconfiguration plans. We noticed that, in the case of DVMS, the time it took to apply a reconfiguration plan largely dominated the time to compute it; however, Entropy spent almost as much time computing as applying reconfiguration plans.

Finally, we used the SimGrid toolkit [CAS 08] to observe how Entropy and DVMS behaved while the workload injected into the VMs fluctuated while they were computing a reconfiguration plan. Thus, we remarked that DVMS consumed little processor resources on each node. We also confirmed that it was able to quickly solve "overloaded node" problems. However, we noted that these experimental parameters penalized Entropy, since the reconfiguration plans became outdated before being applied.

In the next chapter, we will address the limitations of DVMS and the perspectives around it.

Perspectives Around DVMS

In this chapter, we detail the perspectives around the distributed virtual machine scheduler (DVMS).

First, we propose to complete the evaluation of DVMS; we also address some ways to correct its limitations; we finally present the extensions to implement, in order to turn DVMS into a full virtual infrastructure manager.

9.1. Completing the evaluations

The experiments presented in the previous chapter could be completed in several ways, by evaluating the amount of resources consumed by DVMS, using real traces and comparing DVMS with other decentralized approaches.

9.1.1. *Evaluating the amount of resources consumed by DVMS*

First, it could be interesting to evaluate the amount of resources consumed by DVMS to check that it does not have a negative impact on the virtual machines (VMs).

We already know that DVMS uses a single full processor core while computing a reconfiguration plan. Since recent nodes have many cores, it is possible to allocate a core of each worker node to DVMS, so that it can work in ideal conditions without interfering with the VMs.

Moreover, we know that the amount of memory used by DVMS increases to a greater or lesser extent during the computation of a reconfiguration plan, depending on the number of nodes and VMs that are considered; DVMS consumes at most a few dozens of megabytes with Entropy 2 [HER 11], and at most a few hundreds of megabytes with Entropy 1 [HER 09]. Nevertheless, we saw in the previous chapter that DVMS always built small partitions; therefore, its memory footprint is negligible.

However, the cost of network communications is unknown, especially when many events are forwarded to the same node. It would be interesting to check that the bandwidth usage is low in all circumstances, and that network communications do not lead to an increase in processor consumption. Nevertheless, the importance of this factor is relative, since the providers of virtual infrastructure managers generally advise using a dedicated network for the manager; in other words network VMs do not have access to [VMW 11, APA 12, MIC 12].

9.1.2. *Using real traces*

Another way to complement the evaluation of DVMS lies in the use of real traces. In fact, we used a randomly generated workload for our experiments (we ensured reproducibility with a seed); nevertheless, even if DVMS behaved well in most cases, this is not representative of a real system.

The main idea would be to use real traces to inject a relevant workload and check that DVMS can solve (almost) all problems quickly.

However, it is difficult to get real traces, since companies that own them are generally reluctant to share them.

9.1.3. *Comparing DVMS with other decentralized approaches*

To finalize the evaluation of DVMS, it would be good to compare it with other decentralized approaches that can schedule VMs dynamically.

However, only the source code of Snooze [FEL 12c] is currently available, and the other approaches are not always detailed enough to implement a prototype.

9.2. Correcting the limitations

After finishing the evaluation of DVMS, we have several opportunities to overcome the current limitations of the prototype.

9.2.1. *Implementing fault-tolerance*

The first mandatory improvement is to make DVMS fault-tolerant.

9.2.1.1. *Repairing the ring*

Making DVMS fault-tolerant first implies making the ring fault-tolerant. Currently, if a node N_i crashes, an event passing through node N_{i-1} cannot reach node N_{i+1} , unless N_{i-1} knows a shortcut leading to a node N_j $(j \neq i)$.

To preserve the integrity of the ring, we could for instance use the algorithms designed for chord [STO 03]. The main idea is to let each node know not only its neighbor, but also its 2^1 successor, its 2^2 successor and so on until the 2^i successor, i being specified by the administrator; when some part of the ring crashes, network communications can still be performed by passing through a known alive successor.

9.2.1.2. *Pursuing the problem solving procedure*

Having a fault-tolerant ring is not enough; it is also necessary to make the problem solving procedure fault-tolerant.

This implies in particular that:

– the leader of a partition checks if the initiator is alive before trying to solve a problem; if the initiator is faulty, the partition can be destroyed, providing that there is no problem on other nodes involved in the partition;

– the initiator checks that the leader is alive; otherwise, it is necessary to forward the event again to pursue the problem solving procedure;

– each faulty node must be excluded from the partition it was involved in.

9.2.2. *Improving event management*

Besides implementing fault-tolerance, it could be interesting to refine event management.

9.2.2.1. *Building relevant partitions*

To improve event management, it is first worth considering a new way to extend partitions; instead of integrating the first free node that is encountered, it would be better to select a node that is likely to help the problem solving procedure progress.

A first approach could consist of letting close nodes periodically exchange monitoring information regarding their resources; instead of forwarding an event to the first node on the outside of a partition, it would then be possible to select the most relevant node from the monitoring information. However, this approach has two drawbacks: (1) it implies additional network communications and (2) the monitoring information can quickly become outdated.

Another possibility could be to traverse the ring like before, but to integrate a free node inside a partition only if some conditions are met regarding the state of its resources; such a condition, in the case of an "overloaded node" problem, could be that the visited node could host at least one VM running on the initiator.

Finally, another possibility could be to merge/combine partitions that are associated with complementary events, for instance an "overloaded node" event and an "underloaded node" one.

9.2.2.2. *Limiting the size of partitions*

Once partitions are built in a more relevant way, it could be possible to limit their size to ensure the reactivity of DVMS; in fact, we saw in the previous chapter that a few nodes were almost always enough to solve a problem.

Nevertheless, it may not be relevant to limit the size of a partition in all cases; for instance, it should be avoided in the case of an "overloaded node" problem, otherwise it would prevent it from being solved. However, it is particularly interesting in the case of an "underloaded node" event, to prevent the corresponding partition from monopolizing all the nodes of the infrastructure.

9.2.2.3. *Discriminating and prioritizing events*

The previous section introduced the idea of discriminating high priority events, like "overloaded node" ones, that must be solved to avoid penalizing users, from low priority events, like "underloaded node" ones, that are not critical since they aim at optimizing infrastructure utilization.

It could, therefore, be possible to facilitate the growth of partitions associated with "overloaded node" events. For instance, a blocked partition associated with an "overloaded node" event could seize the nodes involved in a growing partition associated with an "underloaded node" event.

9.2.2.4. *Managing new types of events*

One last improvement of DVMS regarding event management could be to let it handle new types of events, for instance linked with the creation of new VMs or with node maintenance.

The creation of a new VM could be handled the same way as an "overloaded node" event; considering that the VM is hosted on a virtual node with no resources, this VM should then be started (and not migrated) on a real node with enough free resources to host it.

Handling a node maintenance could also be implemented by means of an "overloaded node" event; it would be sufficient to specify that the node to put into maintenance mode does not have any free resources left, so that its VMs should be migrated to other nodes.

9.2.3. *Taking account of links between virtual machines*

DVMS considers VMs independently; however, the scheduling algorithms designed for Entropy can manage groups of VMs that are linked with one another.

9.2.3.1. *Specifying affinities and antagonisms*

A first step could be to allow the users to define affinities and antagonisms (1) between the VMs involved in a given group or (2) between a group of VMs and a set of nodes.

These affinities and antagonisms have to be defined on the node in charge of scheduling the VMs; in the context of DVMS, it implies that the leader of each partition knows the placement constraints associated with the VMs it is in charge of. To solve this problem, it could be possible to let each node know the placement constraints associated with each VM it hosts; the leader could then query the nodes to obtain this information.

9.2.3.2. *Executing an action on a group of virtual machines*

Besides enabling the specification of placement constraints, the definition of groups of VMs gives the opportunity to execute a given action on all the VMs belonging to the same group, for instance to suspend or resume them, or to take a snapshot.

The management of groups of VMs could be distributed across DVMS agents by means of a distributed hash table [ROW 01, RAT 01, MAY 02, STO 03, DEC 07]. Note that performing actions on a group of VMs should not interfere with the migrations a leader is likely to order.

9.3. Extending DVMS

In addition to correcting the limitations of DVMS, there are several ways to extend it.

9.3.1. *Managing virtual machine disk images*

A first extension of DVMS could consist of managing the VM disk images.

Relying on a centralized storage system, like Network File System (NFS), should be avoided, since it would prevent DVMS from scaling.

However, it is worth considering a two-layer architecture, similar to the one implemented in OpenStack [OPE 12]. In this approach, nonpersistent VM root partitions would be stored locally, in other words on the nodes hosting VMs; persistent user partitions would be distributed across a set of dedicated storage nodes, to balance the input/output workload between these nodes.

9.3.2. *Managing infrastructures composed of several data centers connected by means of a wide area network*

Another extension of DVMS would consist of managing infrastructures composed of several data centers connected by means of a wide area network.

In this kind of infrastructure, it would be necessary to limit the number of migrations from one data center to another one; in fact, migrating a VM over a wide area network requires not only transferring the content of its memory, but also the whole disk image, which is even more costly as the bandwidth of a wide area network is limited. To decrease the cost of such a migration, it would be possible to leverage deduplication mechanisms [RIT 12].

There are two possibilities to reduce the number of migrations from one data center to another:

– Implementing the bandwidth notion between each node and its neighbor; this requires using a scheduler that can benefit from this information to use in high-priority bandwidth links to migrate VMs; a single ring would then be deployed over the data centers.

– Deploying one ring on each data center; when an event cannot be solved on a data center, the initiator would then query a mediator to forward the event to another data center.

9.3.3. *Integrating DVMS into a full virtual infrastructure manager*

Managing infrastructures composed of several data centers is a beginning, before integrating DVMS into a full virtual infrastructure manager that can especially manage user connections, VM templates, the creation of new VMs and the monitoring of VMs on behalf of users.

This last step should be done by the discovery initiative [LEB 12].

9.4. Conclusion

In this chapter, we have presented several perspectives around DVMS.

We first detailed the evaluations that should be performed to complete the validation of the prototype. They would be related to (1) the consumption in processor, memory and network of DVMS, (2) the use of real traces to inject a real workload into VMs and (3) the comparison of DVMS with another decentralized approach that can dynamically schedule VMs.

Moreover, we identified several solutions to correct the limitations of DVMS regarding fault-tolerance, event management and the handling of links between VMs.

Finally, we presented some opportunities to extend DVMS, to (1) manage VM disk images and (2) infrastructures composed of several data centers connected by means of a wide area network, the final goal being to integrate DVMS into a full virtual infrastructure manager that is currently being designed in the context of the discovery initiative [LEB 12].

Conclusion

In this book, we addressed the management of distributed virtual infrastructures from a software point of view, and more specifically the design of a cooperative and decentralized approach to manage virtual infrastructures.

We first presented the main categories of distributed infrastructures (clusters, data centers and grids) and the frameworks that were commonly used to manage them (user-space frameworks [FOS 06, LAU 06] and distributed operating systems [MUL 90, PIK 95, LOT 05, RIL 06, COR 08]).

We then explained what system virtualization [POP 74, SMI 05] was, and how infrastructure providers and users could benefit from it, especially regarding the mutualization of resources, isolation between users, ease of configuration of work environments and of infrastructure maintenance. We noted that system virtualization contributed to the rise of a new computing paradigm, cloud computing.

After that, we studied the functionalities provided by the main virtual infrastructure managers [NUR 09, SOT 09, VMW 10, VMW 11, APA 12, CIT 12, MIC 12, OPE 12, NIM 13], especially regarding the management of virtual machine lifecycle, scalability, high availability and fault-tolerance. We emphasized the fact that virtual infrastructure managers were highly centralized, which had an impact on scalability, in a context where virtual infrastructures are composed of more and more nodes, up to several tens of thousands [WHO 13].

One way to improve the scalability of virtual machine managers is to decentralize the processing of management tasks, when it is relevant. Such decentralization has already been addressed by research done on distributed operating systems [QUE 11]. Therefore, we studied the similarities between virtual infrastructure managers and distributed operating systems; there are indeed similarities, not only at the node level but also at the infrastructure level, except that virtual infrastructure managers manipulate virtual machines instead of processes. This study enabled us to identify several contributions, especially regarding the decentralization of the dynamic scheduling of virtual machines.

Before focusing on decentralization, we first shed light on the limitations of a centralized approach regarding scalability. On big infrastructures, which are more and more common nowadays, such an approach cannot quickly handle Quality of Service (QoS) violations, and can be slow enough so that a new schedule is outdated before being fully applied. We then studied the related work on the decentralization of virtual machine dynamic scheduling; several hierarchical [FEL 12c] and multiagent [BAR 10, YAZ 10, MAR 11, MAS 11, ROU 11, FEL 12b] approaches had been proposed in the literature, to balance the scheduling task between several nodes, or even all nodes, of an infrastructure; however, we observed that almost all of these approaches were still partially centralized.

We then developed a new approach to schedule virtual machines dynamically and in a decentralized manner in data centers: distributed virtual machine scheduler (DVMS) [QUE 12, QUE 13]. DVMS is deployed as a network of agents organized following a ring topology, and that also cooperate with one another to solve problems related to resource consumption that occur on the infrastructure; DVMS can handle several events simultaneously and independently by dynamically partitioning the infrastructure; the size of each partition is adapted to the complexity of the corresponding event. The ring traversal is optimized, to avoid passing through nodes that are already involved in a partition, and that could not help the problem solving procedure make any more progress. Moreover, we guarantee that a problem will always be solved if a solution exists. We implemented these concepts in a prototype written in the Java programming language. This prototype relies on scheduling algorithms that were designed for the Entropy virtual machine manager [HER 09, HER 11], and that can especially:

– limit the number of migrations, to reduce the cost of applying a new schedule;

– manage sequential dependencies; in other words the fact that migrating a virtual machine could require moving another virtual machine beforehand.

However, this prototype could leverage other scheduling algorithms.

We then described the experimental protocol and the testing environment we used to evaluate the prototype. We addressed the configuration and the functionalities of a framework we specifically designed to test DVMS. We also explained how we deployed this framework on the Grid'5000 test bed [GRI 13], to evaluate DVMS by means of simulations and real experiments; note that the real experiments were facilitated by Flauncher [BAL 12], a tool that enabled us to automate the configuration of nodes and virtual machines, as well as the injection of a workload into virtual machines. In addition, we presented the SimGrid simulation toolkit [CAS 08], and described the advantages of using it instead of deploying our testing framework on Grid'5000.

Afterwards, we analyzed the results obtained during the experiments done with the tools mentioned previously. These results enabled us to compare DVMS with the centralized version of Entropy, either to consolidate virtual machines or to correct "overloaded node" problems. Contrary to previous approaches, DVMS proved to be able to efficiently manage infrastructures involving tens of thousands of virtual machines, and thousands of nodes. DVMS behaved well, and built small partitions to solve the problems it detected; this enabled DVMS to be much more reactive than Entropy, since it solved each problem very quickly. Moreover, DVMS compared favorably with Entropy regarding the virtual machine consolidation rate.

We finally identified several perspectives around DVMS. Additional experiments should be performed to complement the validation of DVMS, to evaluate its use in resources, how it behaves with real traces, and how it compares to other decentralized approaches. Furthermore, several corrections should be made, especially regarding fault-tolerance and event management. The final goal is to integrate DVMS in a full virtual infrastructure manager, which is currently designed in the context of the discovery initiative [LEB 12].

Bibliography

[ADA 12] ADAPTIVE COMPUTING ENTERPRISES, Inc., TORQUE 4.0.2 Administrator Guide, 2012.

[ADV 08] ADVANCED MICRO DEVICES, Inc., AMD-V Nested Paging, Sunnyvale, CA, July 2008.

[AND 04] ANDERSON D.P., "BOINC: a system for public-resource computing and storage", *GRID '04: Proceedings of the 5th IEEE/ACM International Workshop on Grid Computing*, IEEE Computer Society, Washington, DC, November 2004.

[APA 12] APACHE SOFTWARE FOUNDATION, Apache CloudStack 4.0.0-incubating Administrator's Guide, Forest Hill, MD, May 2012.

[ARC 09] ARCANGELI A., EIDUS I., WRIGHT C., "Increasing memory density by using KSM", *OLS '09: Proceedings of the Linux Symposium*, pp. 19–28, July 2009.

[AWS 13] AMAZON WEB SERVICES, available at http://aws.amazon.com, January 2013.

[AZU 13] Windows Azure, available at http://www.windowsazure.com, January 2013.

[BAL 12] BALOUEK D., CARPEN AMARIE A., CHARRIER G., *et al.*, Adding virtualization capabilities to Grid'5000, Report no. RR-8026, INRIA, July 2012.

[BAR 03] BARHAM P., DRAGOVIC B., FRASER K., *et al.*, "Xen and the art of virtualization", *SOSP '03: Proceedings of the 19th ACM Symposium on Operating Systems Principles*, New York, NY, ACM, pp. 164–177, October 2003.

[BAR 10] BARBAGALLO D., DI NITTO E., DUBOIS D., *et al.*, "A bio-inspired algorithm for energy optimization in a self-organizing data center", in WEYNS D., MALEK S., DE LEMOS R., *et al.*, (eds.), *Self-Organizing Architectures*, Lecture Notes in Computer Science, Springer, Berlin/Heidelberg, Germany, vol. 6090, pp. 127–151, 2010.

[BEL 05] BELLARD F., "QEMU, a fast and portable dynamic translator", *ATEC'05: Proceedings of the Annual Conference on USENIX Annual Technical Conference*, USENIX Association, Berkeley, CA, pp. 41–46, April 2005.

[BHA 08] BHATTIPROLU S., BIEDERMAN E.W., HALLYN S., *et al.*, "Virtual servers and checkpoint/restart in mainstream Linux", *SIGOPS Operating Systems Review*, ACM, vol. 42, no. 5, pp. 104–113, July 2008.

[BUY 01] BUYYA R., CORTES T., JIN H., "Single system image", *International Journal of High Performance Computing Applications*, vol. 15, no. 2, pp. 124–135, May 2001.

[CAP 05] CAPIT N., DA COSTA G., GEORGIOU Y., *et al.*, "A batch scheduler with high level components", *CCGrid '05: Proceedings of the 5th IEEE International Symposium on Cluster Computing and the Grid*, IEEE Computer Society, Washington, DC, vol. 2, pp. 776–783, May 2005.

[CAS 08] CASANOVA H., LEGRAND A., QUINSON M., "SimGrid: a generic framework for large-scale distributed experiments", *UKSIM '08: Proceedings of the 10th International Conference on Computer Modeling and Simulation*, IEEE Computer Society, Washington, DC, pp. 126–131, April 2008.

[CAV 09] CAVILLA H.A.L., WHITNEY J.A., SCANNELL A.M., *et al.*, "SnowFlock: rapid virtual machine cloning for cloud computing", *EuroSys'09: Proceedings of the 4th ACM European Conference on Computer Systems*, ACM, New York, NY, pp. 1–12, 2009.

[CER 09] CERLING T., BULLER J., ENSTALL C., *et al.*, *Mastering Microsoft Virtualization*, Wiley Publishing, Indianapolis, IN, December 2009.

[CFS 13] CFS Scheduler, available at http://www.kernel.org/doc/Documentation/scheduler/sched-design-CFS.txt, January 2013.

[CHA 85] CHANDY K.M., LAMPORT L., "Distributed snapshots: determining global states of distributed systems", *ACM Transactions on Computer Systems*, vol. 3, no. 1, pp. 63–75, February 1985.

[CHA 09] CHAPMAN M., HEISER G., "vNUMA: a virtual shared-memory multiprocessor", *ATEC'09: Proceedings of the USENIX Annual Technical Conference*, USENIX Association, pp. 15–28, June 2009.

[CHI 07] CHISNALL D., *The Definitive Guide to the Xen Hypervisor*, Prentice Hall PTR, Upper Saddle River, NJ, 2007.

[CIT 12] CITRIX SYSTEMS, Inc., Citrix XenServer 6.0 Administrator's Guide, Santa Clara, CA, March 2012.

[CLA 05] CLARK C., FRASER K., HAND S., *et al.*, "Live migration of virtual machines", *NSDI'05: Proceedings of the 2nd Conference on Symposium on Networked Systems Design and Implementation*, USENIX Association, Berkeley, CA, pp. 273–286, May 2005.

[COR 08] CORTES T., FRANKE C., JÉGOU Y., *et al.*, XtreemOS: a vision for a grid operating System, Report, XtreemOS, May 2008.

[CRE 81] CREASY R.J., "The origin of the VM/370 time-sharing system", *IBM Journal of Research and Development*, vol. 25, no. 5, pp. 483–490, September 1981.

[DEC 07] DECANDIA G., HASTORUN D., JAMPANI M., *et al.*, "Dynamo: amazon's highly available key-value store", *SIGOPS Operating Systems Review*, vol. 41, no. 6, pp. 205–220, October 2007.

[EGI 13] EGI – European Grid Infrastructure – towards a sustainable infrastructure, available at http://www.egi.eu/, January 2013.

[ERI 09] ERIKSSON J., Virtualization, isolation and emulation in a Linux environment, Master's Thesis, Umea University, SE-901 87 UMEA, Sweden, April 2009.

[ESK 96] ESKICIOGLU M.R., "A comprehensive bibliography of distributed shared memory", *SIGOPS Operating Systems Review*, ACM, vol. 30, no. 1, pp. 71–96, January 1996.

[EUC 12] EUCALYPTUS SYSTEMS, Inc., Eucalyptus 3.1.1 Administration Guide, Goleta, CA, https://www.eucalyptus.com/docs/eucalyptus/3.1/ag-3.1.1.pdf, August 2012.

[FED 01] FEDAK G., GERMAIN C., NERI V. *et al.*, "XtremWeb: a generic global computing system", *CCGRID '01: Proceedings of the 1st IEEE/ACM International Symposium on Cluster Computing and the Grid*, pp. 582–587, May 2001.

[FEL 12a] FELLER E., MORIN C., "Autonomous and energy-aware management of large-scale cloud infrastructures", *IPDPSW '12: Proceedings of the IEEE 26th International Parallel and Distributed Processing Symposium Workshops PhD Forum*, IEEE Computer Society, Washington, DC, pp. 2542–2545, May 2012.

[FEL 12b] FELLER E., MORIN C., ESNAULT A., "A case for fully decentralized dynamic VM consolidation in clouds", *CloudCom '12: 4th IEEE International Conference on Cloud Computing Technology and Science*, IEEE Computer Society, Washington, DC, December 2012.

[FEL 12c] FELLER E., RILLING L., MORIN C., "Snooze: a scalable and autonomic virtual machine management framework for private clouds", *CCGRID '12: Proceedings of the 2012 12th IEEE/ACM International Symposium on Cluster, Cloud and Grid Computing*, IEEE Computer Society, Washington, DC, pp. 482–489, May 2012.

[FOR 13] Force.com, available at http://www.force.com/, January 2013.

[FOS 06] FOSTER I.T., "Globus toolkit version 4: software for service-oriented systems", *Journal of Computer Science and Technology*, vol. 21, no. 4, pp. 513–520, July 2006.

[FOS 08] FOSTER I., ZHAO Y., RAICU I., *et al.*, "Cloud computing and grid computing 360-degree compared", *GCE '08: Proceedings of Grid Computing Environments Workshop*, IEEE Computer Society, Washington, DC, pp. 1–10, November 2008.

[FRA 13] FRANCE GRILLES, Des solutions innovantes répondant à la croissance exponentielle des besoins de stockage et de traitement des données dans de nombreuses disciplines scientifiques, available at http://www.france-grilles.fr/?lang=en, January 2013.

[FUT 13] FUTUREGRID PORTAL, available at https://portal.futuregrid.org/, January 2013.

[GAE 13] GOOGLE APP ENGINE, available at https://developers.google.com/appengine/, January 2013.

[GOS 02] GOSCINSKI A., HOBBS M., SILCOCK J., "GENESIS: an efficient, transparent and easy to use cluster operating system", *Parallel Computing*, vol. 28, no. 4, pp. 557–606, April 2002.

[GRI 13] Grid'5000, a scientific instrument designed to support experiment-driven research in all areas of computer science related to parallel, large-scale or distributed computing and networking, available at https://www.grid5000.fr, January 2013.

[HAN 05] HAND S., WARFIELD A., FRASER K., *et al.*, "Are virtual machine monitors microkernels done right?", *HOTOS '05: Proceedings of the 10th Conference on Hot Topics in Operating Systems*, USENIX Association, Berkeley, CA, vol. 10, June 2005.

[HEI 06] HEISER G., UHLIG V., LEVASSEUR J., "Are virtual-machine monitors microkernels done right?", *SIGOPS Operating Systems Review*, vol. 40, no. 1, pp. 95–99, January 2006.

[HEM 13] HEMERA, available at https://www.grid5000.fr/mediawiki/index.php/Hemera, January 2013.

[HER 09] HERMENIER F., LORCA X., MENAUD J.M., *et al.*, "Entropy: a consolidation manager for clusters", *VEE'09: Proceedings of the ACM SIGPLAN/SIGOPS International Conference on Virtual Execution Environments*, ACM, New York, NY, pp. 41–50, March 2009.

[HER 10] HERMENIER F., LÈBRE A., MENAUD J.-M., "Cluster-wide context switch of virtualized jobs", *VTDC '10: Proceedings of the 4th International Workshop on Virtualization Technologies in Distributed Computing*, ACM, New York, NY, June 2010.

[HER 11] HERMENIER F., DEMASSEY S., LORCA X., "Bin repacking scheduling in virtualized datacenters", *CP '11: Proceedings of the 17th International Conference on Principles and Practice of Constraint Programming*, Springer, Berlin/Heidelberg, Germany, pp. 27–41, 2011.

[HIR 11] HIROFUCHI T., NAKADA H., ITOH S., *et al.*, "Reactive consolidation of virtual machines enabled by postcopy live migration", *VTDC '11: Proceedings of the 5th International Workshop on Virtualization Technologies in Distributed Computing*, ACM, New York, NY, pp. 11–18, June 2011.

[HYP 13] HYPER-V, Configure Memory and Processors, available at http://technet.microsoft.com/en-us/library/cc742470.aspx, January 2013.

[KAD 13] KADEPLOY, scalable, efficient and reliable deployment tool for clusters and Grid computing, available at http://kadeploy3.gforge.inria.fr/, January 2013.

[KAV 13] KaVLAN, available at https://www.grid5000.fr/mediawiki/index.php/KaVLAN, January 2013.

[KIV 07] KIVITY A., KAMAY Y., LAOR D., *et al.*, "kvm: the Linux virtual machine monitor", *OLS '07: Proceedings of the Linux Symposium*, vol. 1, pp. 225–230, June 2007.

[KOT 10] KOTSOVINOS E., "Virtualization: blessing or curse?", *Queue*, vol. 8, no. 11, pp. 40–46, November 2010.

[LAN 10] LANGE J., PEDRETTI K., HUDSON T., *et al.*, "Palacios and Kitten: new high performance operating systems for scalable virtualized and native supercomputing", *IPDPS '10: Proceedings of the 24th IEEE International Parallel and Distributed Processing Symposium*, IEEE Computer Society, Washington, DC, April 2010.

[LAU 06] LAURE E., FISHER S.M., FROHNER A., *et al.*, "Programming the grid with gLite", *Computational Methods in Science and Technology*, vol. 12, no. 1, pp. 33–45, 2006.

[LEB 12] LEBRE A., ANEDDA P., GAGGERO M., *et al.*, "DISCOVERY, beyond the clouds", *Euro-Par 2011: Parallel Processing Workshops*, Lecture Notes in Computer Science, Springer, Berlin/Heidelberg, Germany, vol. 7156, pp. 446–456, 2012.

[LEU 04] LEUNG J.Y.T., *Handbook of Scheduling: Algorithms, Models, and Performance Analysis*, Computer and Information Science, CRC Press LLC, Boca Raton, FL, 2004.

[LIB 13] LIBVIRT: The virtualization API, available at http://libvirt.org/, January 2013.

[LIG 03] LIGNERIS B.D., SCOTT S.L., NAUGHTON T., *et al.*, "Open source cluster application resources (OSCAR): design, implementation and interest for the [computer] scientific community", *HPCS '03: Proceedings of 17th Annual International Symposium on High Performance Computing Systems and Applications*, NRC Research Press, Ottawa, Canada, May 2003.

[LIN 99] LINDHOLM T., YELLIN F., *Java Virtual Machine Specification*, 2nd edition, Addison-Wesley Longman Publishing Co., Inc., Boston, MA, 1999.

[LOT 05] LOTTIAUX R., GALLARD P., VALLEE G., *et al.*, "OpenMosix, OpenSSI and Kerrighed: a comparative study", *CCGRID '05: Proceedings of the 5th IEEE International Symposium on Cluster Computing and the Grid*, IEEE Computer Society, Washington, DC, vol. 2, pp. 1016–1023, May 2005.

[LOW 09] LOWE S., *Introducing VMware vSphere 4*, 1st edition, Wiley Publishing Inc., Indianapolis, IN, September 2009.

[MAR 11] MARZOLLA M., BABAOGLU O., PANZIERI F., "Server consolidation in Clouds through gossiping", *WoWMoM '11: Proceedings of the 12th IEEE International Symposium on a World of Wireless, Mobile and Multimedia Networks*, IEEE Computer Society, Washington, DC, pp. 1–6, June 2011.

[MAS 11] MASTROIANNI C., MEO M., PAPUZZO G., "Self-economy in cloud data centers: statistical assignment and migration of virtual machines", *Euro-Par '11: Proceedings of the 17th International Conference on Parallel Processing*, Springer, Berlin/Heidelberg, Germany, vol. 1, 2011.

[MAY 02] MAYMOUNKOV P., MAZIÈRES D., "Kademlia: a peer-to-peer information system based on the XOR metric", in DRUSCHEL P., KAASHOEK F., ROWSTRON A., (eds.), *Peer-to-Peer Systems*, Lecture Notes in Computer Science, Springer, Berlin/Heidelberg, Germany, vol. 2429, pp. 53–65, 2002.

[MEN 13] MENAGE P., JACKSON P., LAMETER C., "cgroups", available at http://www.kernel.org/doc/Documentation/cgroups/cgroups.txt, January 2013.

[MIC 12] MICROSOFT CORPORATION, Redmond, WA, System Center 2012, Virtual Machine Manager Technical Documentation, http://www.microsoft.com/en-us/download/details.aspx?id=6346, April 2012.

[MIL 00] MILOJICIC D.S., DOUGLIS F., PAINDAVEINE Y., *et al.*, "Process migration", *ACM Computing Surveys*, vol. 32, no. 3, pp. 241–299, September 2000.

[MUL 90] MULLENDER S.J., VAN ROSSUM G., TANANBAUM A.S., *et al.*, "Amoeba: a distributed operating system for the 1990s", *Computer*, vol. 23, no. 5, pp. 44–53, May 1990.

[NIM 13] NIMBUS 2.10, available at http://www.nimbusproject.org/docs/2.10/, January 2013.

[NUR 09] NURMI D., WOLSKI R., GRZEGORCZYK C.,"The eucalyptus open-source cloud-computing system", *CCGRID '09: Proceedings of the 9th IEEE/ACM International Symposium on Cluster Computing and the Grid*, IEEE Computer Society, Washington, DC, vol. 0, pp. 124–131, May 2009.

[NUS 09] NUSSBAUM L., ANHALT F., MORNARD O., *et al.*, "Linux-based virtualization for HPC clusters", *OLS '09: Proceedings of the Linux Symposium*, pp. 221–234, July 2009.

[OPE 12] OPENSTACK, LLC, OpenStack Compute Administration Manual, folsom edition, San Antonio, TX, http://docs.openstack.org/admin-guide-cloud/content/, November 2012.

[OPE 13] OPENNEBULA 3.8, available at http://archives.opennebula.org/ documentation:archives:rel3.8, January 2013.

[OSG 13] THE OPEN SCIENCE GRID, available at https://www. opensciencegrid.org/bin/view, January 2013.

[PAJ 13] PAJÉ VISUALIZATION TOOL, analysis of execution traces, available at http://paje.sourceforge.net/, January 2013.

[PAR 11] PARK E., EGGER B., LEE J., "Fast and space-efficient virtual machine checkpointing", *VEE '11: Proceedings of the 7th ACM SIGPLAN/SIGOPS International Conference on Virtual Execution Environments*, ACM, New York, NY, March 2011.

[PIK 95] PIKE R., PRESOTTO D., DORWARD S.,"Plan 9 from Bell Labs", *Computing Systems*, vol. 8, pp. 221–254, 1995.

[POP 74] POPEK G.J., GOLDBERG R.P., "Formal requirements for virtualizable third generation architectures", *Communications of the ACM*, vol. 17, no. 7, pp. 412–421, July 1974.

[PRP 13] PRPI M., LANDMANN R., SILAS D., "Red Hat Enterprise Linux 6 Resource Management Guide", available at https://access.redhat.com/knowledge/docs/en-US/Red_Hat_Enterprise_Linux/6/html-single/Resource_Management_Guide/index.html, January 2013.

[QUE 11] QUESNEL F., LÈBRE A., "Operating systems and virtualization frameworks: from local to distributed similarities", *PDP '11: Proceedings of the 19th Euromicro International Conference on Parallel, Distributed and Network-Based Computing*, IEEE Computer Society, Los Alamitos, CA, pp. 495–502, February 2011.

[QUE 12] QUESNEL F., LÈBRE A., "Cooperative dynamic scheduling of virtual machines in distributed systems", *Euro-Par 2011: Parallel Processing Workshops*, Lecture Notes in Computer Science, Springer, Berlin/Heidelberg, Germany, vol. 7156, pp. 457–466, 2012.

[QUE 13] QUESNEL F., LÈBRE A., SÜDHOLT M., "Cooperative and reactive scheduling in large-scale virtualized platforms with DVMS", *Concurrency and Computation: Practice and Experience*, John Wiley & Sons, vol. 25, no. 12, pp. 1643–1655, August 2013.

[RAT 01] RATNASAMY S., FRANCIS P., HANDLEY M., *et al.*, "A scalable content-addressable network", *SIGCOMM'01: Proceedings of the Conference on Applications, Technologies, Architectures, and Protocols for Computer Communications*, SIGCOMM '01, ACM, New York, NY, pp. 161–172, August 2001.

[RIL 06] RILLING L., "Vigne: towards a self-healing grid operating system", *Proceedings of Euro-Par*, Lecture Notes in Computer Science, Springer, Berlin/Heidelberg, Germany, vol. 4128, pp. 437–447, August 2006.

[RIT 12] RITEAU P., MORIN C., PRIOL T., "Shrinker: efficient live migration of virtual clusters over wide area networks", *Concurrency and Computation: Practice and Experience*, John Wiley & Sons, 2012.

[ROB 00] ROBIN J.S., IRVINE C.E., "Analysis of the Intel Pentium's ability to support a secure virtual machine monitor", *SSYM '00: Proceedings of the 9th Conference on USENIX Security Symposium*, USENIX Association, Berkeley, CA, pp. 129–144, August 2000.

[ROS 07] ROSCOE T., ELPHINSTONE K., HEISER G., "Hype and virtue", *HOTOS '07: Proceedings of the 11th USENIX Workshop on Hot Topics in Operating Systems*, USENIX Association, Berkeley, CA, pp. 1–6, May 2007.

[ROT 94] ROTITHOR H.G., "Taxonomy of dynamic task scheduling schemes in distributed computing systems", *IEE Proceedings – Computers and Digital Techniques*, vol. 141, no. 1, pp. 1–10, January 1994.

[ROU 11] ROUZAUD CORNABAS J., "A distributed and collaborative dynamic load balancer for virtual machine", *Euro-Par 2010 Parallel Processing Workshops*, Lecture Notes in Computer Science, Springer, Berlin/Heidelberg, Germany, vol. 6586, pp. 641–648, August 2011.

[ROW 01] ROWSTRON A., DRUSCHEL P., "Pastry: scalable, decentralized object location, and routing for large-scale peer-to-peer systems", *Middleware*, Lecture Notes in Computer Science, Springer, Berlin/Heidelberg, Germany, vol. 2218, pp. 329–350, 2001.

[RUS 07] RUSSEL R., "lguest: Implementing the little Linux hypervisor", *OLS '07: Proceedings of the Linux Symposium*, vol. 2, pp. 173–178, June 2007.

[SAL 13] Salesforce.com – CRM and cloud computing, available at http://www.salesforce.com/, January 2013.

[SCH 13] LINUX SCHEDULING DOMAINS, available at http://www.kernel.org/doc/Documentation/scheduler/sched-domains.txt, January 2013.

[SET 13] SETI@HOME, available at http://setiathome.berkeley.edu/, January 2013.

[SIL 98] SILBERSCHATZ A., GALVIN P.B., *Operating System Concepts*, 5th edition, Addison-Wesley, Reading, MA, August 1998.

[SIM 13] SIMGRID: versatile simulation of distributed systems, available at http://simgrid.gforge.inria.fr/, January 2013.

[SMI 05] SMITH J.E., NAIR R., *Virtual Machines: Versatile Platforms for Systems and Processes*, Morgan Kaufmann Publishers, San Francisco, CA, 2005.

[SOL 07] SOLTESZ S., PÖTZL H., FIUCZYNSKI M.E., *et al.*, "Container-based operating system virtualization: a scalable, high-performance alternative to hypervisors", *EuroSys'07: Proceedings of the 2nd ACM SIGOPS/EuroSys European Conference on Computer Systems*, ACM, New York, NY, vol. 41, pp. 275–287, March 2007.

[SOT 09] SOTOMAYOR B., MONTERO R.S., LLORENTE I.M., *et al.*, "Virtual infrastructure management in private and hybrid clouds", *IEEE Internet Computing*, IEEE Educational Activities Department, vol. 13, no. 5, pp. 14–22, September 2009.

[STA 08] STALLINGS W., *Operating Systems Internals and Design Principles*, 6th edition, Prentice-Hall, Upper Saddle River, NJ, July 2008.

[STE 10] STEINBERG U., KAUER B., "NOVA: a microhypervisor-based secure virtualization architecture", *EuroSys '10: Proceedings of the 5th European Conference on Computer Systems*, ACM, New York, NY, pp. 209–222, April 2010.

[STO 03] STOICA I., MORRIS R., LIBEN-NOWELL D.,"Chord: a scalable peer-to-peer lookup protocol for internet applications", *IEEE/ACM Transactions on Networking*, IEEE Press, vol. 11, no. 1, pp. 17–32, February 2003.

[TAK 13] Taktuk, Adaptive large scale remote executions deployment, available at http://taktuk.gforge.inria.fr/, January 2013.

[TAN 01] TANENBAUM A.S., *Modern Operating Systems*, 2nd edition, Prentice-Hall, Upper Saddle River, NJ, March 2001.

[THA 05] THAIN D., TANNENBAUM T., LIVNY M., "Distributed computing in practice: the Condor experience", *Concurrency and Computation: Practice and Experience*, John Wiley & Sons, vol. 17, pp. 323–356, February 2005.

[UHL 05] UHLIG R., NEIGER G., RODGERS D., *et al.*, "Intel virtualization technology", *Computer*, IEEE Computer Society Press, vol. 38, no. 5, pp. 48–56, May 2005.

[VMW 09] VMware, inc., VMware vSphere 4: The CPU Scheduler in VMware ESX 4, Palo Alto, CA, http://www.vmware.com/files/pdf/perf-vsphere-cpu_scheduler.pdf, 2009.

[VMW 10] VMware, Inc., Palo Alto, CA, USA, VMware vCloud Architecting a vCloud, 2010.

[VMW 11] VMware, Inc., Palo Alto, CA, USA, VMware vSphere Basics, 2009-2011.

[VOG 08] VOGELS W., "Beyond server consolidation", *Queue*, ACM, vol. 6, no. 1, pp. 20–26, 2008.

[VSM 13] VERSATILE SMP (vSMP) Architecture, available at http://www.scalemp.com/architecture, January 2013.

[WAL 02] WALDSPURGER C.A., "Memory resource management in VMware ESX server", *SIGOPS Operating Systems Review*, ACM, vol. 36, no. SI, pp. 181–194, December 2002.

[WHO 13] Who Has the Most Web Servers?, available at http://www.datacenterknowledge.com/archives/2009/05/14/whos-got-the-most-web-servers/, January 2013.

[WIN 13] WINDOWS SCHEDULING, available at http://msdn.microsoft.com/en-us/library/windows/desktop/ms685096.aspx, January 2013.

[WIC 13] WLCG, Worldwide LHC Computing Grid, available at http://wlcg.web.cern.ch/, January 2013.

[WOO 09] WOOD T., LEVIN G.T., SHENOY P., *et al.*, "Memory buddies: exploiting page sharing for smart colocation in virtualized data centers", *SIGOPS Operating Systems Review*, ACM, vol. 43, no. 3, pp. 27–36, July 2009.

[XSE 13] XSEDE, Extreme Science and Engineering Discovery Environment, available at https://www.xsede.org/home, January 2013.

[YAZ 10] YAZIR Y.O., MATTHEWS C., FARAHBOD R., *et al.*, "Dynamic resource allocation in computing clouds using distributed multiple criteria decision analysis", *Cloud '10: IEEE 3rd International Conference on Cloud Computing*, IEEE Computer Society, Los Alamitos, CA, pp. 91–98, July 2010.

List of Tables

List of Figures

Index

Other titles from

in

Computer Engineering

2014

OUSSALAH Mourad Chabane
Software Architecture 1

OUSSALAH Mourad Chabane
Software Architecture 2

TOUATI Sid, DE DINECHIN Benoit
Advanced Backend Optimization

2013

ANDRÉ Etienne, SOULAT Romain
The Inverse Method: Parametric Verification of Real-time Embedded Systems

BOULANGER Jean-Louis
Safety Management for Software-based Equipment

DELAHAYE Daniel, PUECHMOREL Stéphane
Modeling and Optimization of Air Traffic

FRANCOPOULO Gil
LMF — Lexical Markup Framework

2011

BICHOT Charles-Edmond, SIARRY Patrick
Graph Partitioning

BOULANGER Jean-Louis
Static Analysis of Software: The Abstract Interpretation

CAFERRA Ricardo
Logic for Computer Science and Artificial Intelligence

HOMES Bernard
Fundamentals of Software Testing

KORDON Fabrice, HADDAD Serge, PAUTET Laurent, PETRUCCI Laure
Distributed Systems: Design and Algorithms

KORDON Fabrice, HADDAD Serge, PAUTET Laurent, PETRUCCI Laure
Models and Analysis in Distributed Systems

LORCA Xavier
Tree-based Graph Partitioning Constraint

TRUCHET Charlotte, ASSAYAG Gerard
Constraint Programming in Music

VICAT-BLANC PRIMET Pascale *et al.*
Computing Networks: From Cluster to Cloud Computing

2010

AUDIBERT Pierre
Mathematics for Informatics and Computer Science

BABAU Jean-Philippe *et al.*
Model Driven Engineering for Distributed Real-Time Embedded Systems 2009

BOULANGER Jean-Louis
Safety of Computer Architectures

MONMARCHÉ Nicolas *et al.*
Artificial Ants

PASCHOS Vangelis Th
Combinatorial Optimization and Theoretical Computer Science: Interfaces and Perspectives

WALDNER Jean-Baptiste
Nanocomputers and Swarm Intelligence

2007

BENHAMOU Frédéric, JUSSIEN Narendra, O'SULLIVAN Barry
Trends in Constraint Programming

JUSSIEN Narendra
A to Z of Sudoku

2006

BABAU Jean-Philippe *et al.*
From MDD Concepts to Experiments and Illustrations – DRES 2006

HABRIAS Henri, FRAPPIER Marc
Software Specification Methods

MURAT Cecile, PASCHOS Vangelis Th
Probabilistic Combinatorial Optimization on Graphs

PANETTO Hervé, BOUDJLIDA Nacer
Interoperability for Enterprise Software and Applications 2006 / IFAC-IFIP I-ESA'2006

2005

GÉRARD Sébastien *et al.*
Model Driven Engineering for Distributed Real Time Embedded Systems

PANETTO Hervé
Interoperability of Enterprise Software and Applications 2005